THE KNITTED
SLIPPER BOOK

THE KNITTED SLIPPER BOOK

Slippers and House Shoes for the Entire Family

KATIE STARTZMAN

Photographs by Mika Nakanishi
(unless otherwise noted)

STC Craft | A Melanie Falick Book

stewart tabori & chang
An imprint of ABRAMS

Published in 2013 by Stewart, Tabori & Chang
An imprint of ABRAMS

Clothing and accessories for *The Knitted Slipper Book* were provided by:

American Apparel	HUG†OH Harajuku	Optical Tailor Cradle Aoyama
www.store.americanapparel.co.jp	www.hug-harajuku.com	www.cradle.ne.jp
tel. +81-3-6418-5403	tel. +81-3-3478-5018	tel. +81-3-6418-0577

Cataloging-in-Publication Data has been applied for and may be obtained from the Library of Congress.
ISBN: 978-1-61769-058-7

Editor: Melanie Falick
Designer: Miao Wang
Production Manager: Tina Cameron

The text of this book was composed in Johnston ITC.

Printed and bound in Hong Kong, China
10 9 8 7 6 5 4 3 2 1

Stewart, Tabori & Chang books are available at special discounts when purchased in quantity for premiums and promotions as well as fundraising or educational use. Special editions can also be created to specification. For details, contact specialsales@abramsbooks.com or the address below.

THE ART OF BOOKS SINCE 1949
115 West 18th Street
New York, NY 10011
www.abramsbooks.com

{ FOR MY GRANDMOTHERS, JUNE AND CLAIRE }

CONTENTS

INTRODUCTION

I learned to knit from books when I was in my early twenties. I used dime-store yarn and slippery metal needles and made multiple uneven swatches until, one day, I learned that a family friend was having a baby. Excited by the news, I bought a pattern for garter-stitch booties and then—very, very slowly—followed it. Back then I had no idea that those booties were a foreshadowing of my future.

I grew up in rural New York and then Pennsylvania with my three siblings and my parents. My mom and dad are the kind of people who can do anything: make a showplace of a two-hundred-year-old house, tend a huge garden, and sew Halloween costumes for four kids, all with grace and love on a shoestring budget. With no television in sight and farm fields for neighbors, my twin sister, Laura, and I, along with my brother and sister, Josh and Abby, would build forts, bridges, and dollhouses. I even remember trying our hand at wallpapering our basement. My mom let us make messes and generously shared her art supplies (but not her fabric scissors!), and my dad kept his cool if we left his hammer out in the rain. It was a wonderful way to grow up and, of course, I didn't realize how unique and special it was until I was an adult.

After high school I headed to Berea College in Kentucky, which is a small liberal arts college that was founded before the Civil War on the ideals of equality and affordable education. Today, students from Appalachia and around the world attend Berea tuition-free. A DIY-and-sustainability ethos imbues everything that happens there. All students are required to work in jobs around campus, such as tending the college farm, preparing food in the cafeteria, supporting office staff, and maintaining the grounds. I spent a couple of years working in the office of the Student Crafts program, where students make pottery, weave linens, make brooms, and do woodworking (the wares are then sold to raise money for the capital fund). Even back then I appreciated the desire to preserve and share these traditional crafts. My husband is a Berea native, so now this little Kentucky town is my home too. I'm proud to live in a community of creative folks who value sustainability and self-sufficiency.

My desire to live simply often intersects with my creative pursuits. Born partly from a sense of thrift, but mostly from rampant curiosity, I enjoy learning how to create things that make me self-sufficient. Often, after I complete my admittedly obsessive research and mess around with my pursuit for a while, I'm ready to move on to some other kind of puzzle. This was true when I was raising Angora goats, learning to make baskets, and sculpting clay and sand to make a pizza oven. (There are lots of stories about my fascinations old and new on the blog I share with my twin sister, Laura, at www.duofiberworks.com). It's also true of my desire to make shoes and sandals. It's easy enough to find a decent pair of jeans at a thrift store, knit a sweater, or sew a simple dress. But shoes are the weakest link in a low-impact clothing diet. Shoes are largely made in faraway countries from energy-consumptive materials, or they are carefully made by hand but are out of my financial reach. It is deeply satisfying to begin with a stiff, unfinished piece of leather and end up with a pair of supple, stylish sandals. They are simply leather and thread with a bit of glue, but they become so much more with the mastery of skills and the addition of time. Knitted slippers possess a similar kind of magic: They are nothing more than yarn, time, and skill, combined to make

Left to right: Recycled Fringe Slippers (page 61), Pom-Pom Flats (page 41), and Sunday Morning Scuffs (page 73).

something lovely and useful. Crafting handmade shoes is something that takes years to master, and I'm not sure how far I'd like to pursue my interests there. However, a pair of knitted slippers can be made in a weekend, and they are longer-lasting and more special than store-bought.

Throughout my various creative endeavors, something about knitting—and particularly felting—has stuck with me. The myriad challenges and possibilities of these techniques have kept me captivated. Soon after I began to knit, I learned about felting from Beverly Galeskas's classic book, *Felted Knits*. I still have the funky green bag I knitted and felted, and I also made a few pairs of her cleverly designed clogs. I was transfixed by the alchemical transformation of loose, floppy knitting into firm, durable, sculptural shapes. Because I had two small boys at the time, I set out to make some knitted and felted toys that took advantage of these most excellent qualities. That's how I got my start as a designer, puzzling out how to make a small toy horse that maintained its proportions after felting. I soon realized that the same features that made felted toys so successful would translate to lovely slippers.

Felted knitting is ideal for slippers thanks to its smooth surface, sturdy nature, and seamless look. Many of the projects in this book are my explorations into how best to use this technique to make comfortable, long-lasting slippers. But because all slipper styles aren't suited to felting (and because sometimes I just want to knit and be done), I've also included "plain" knitted slippers.

Slippers are nice to wear on Saturday mornings, curled up by the woodstove, but they aren't just winter-weather warmers. Many people prefer to remove their shoes at the door of their homes, keeping outside grime out of their living space, and the slippers in this book serve as excellent house shoes. I think of them as shoes for your life at home. Just as I have more than one pair of shoes, I enjoy having a couple pairs of slippers around. My Trim Clogs (page 55) are my go-to pair for the weekends, and I'm sometimes guilty of borrowing my husband's roomy and extra-warm Woolly

Left: Chunky Slipper Boots (page 77).

Wellies (page 33). My red Cotton Loafers (page 137) are great in the summer, as the jute sole is sturdy enough to venture down to my garden and the cotton is light and cool in the heat. I prefer my embellished Options Flats (page 99) for when we're entertaining and I'm going to be on my feet, as they are light and shoelike. My Ankle Fringe Boots (page 119), with their sturdy leather sole, push the boundaries of slippers, as I often sneak out of the house in them to drop off my kids at school or grab a latte. And for that home-away-from-home-feeling, I always pack my Travel Slippers (page 127) when I am going out of town.

There are many more designs I'm still planning to make for family and friends, as well as a collection of House Clogs (page 133) in different colors to place by my front door for guests. As I write this I have on my needles a pair of Inside-Out Slipper Socks (page 95) for my youngest son. They are his favorite because they are easy to pull on and their height makes them extra cozy. And I've got a request from my nephew to knit him a pair of Lace-Up Boots (page 65). He likes them best because they resemble the work boots his forest ranger dad wears every day.

Left to right: Tassel Loafers (page 107), Lace-Up Boots (page 65), and Pull-On "Puddle" Boots (page 129).

Sometimes people are hesitant to try knitting and felting because they are worried that they won't be able to control the felting process. But in this book I teach you how to felt by hand, which removes the riskiness of felting by machine, and makes it possible to sculpt the pieces to your specifications. You actually have more control because, after the knitting is completed, you have the opportunity to felt it down to just the right size and shape. So if you're feeling a little hesitant about felting, please trust me and give it a try. I think you'll be surprised by its meditative qualities. Hand-felting is calming and absorbing, and the magical nature of the fabric transforming before your eyes is satisfying and delightful.

The work of writing this book and sharing my knowledge about how to make handmade slippers has been a privilege, and I will feel richly rewarded if you enjoy following my patterns. I hope you wear and share the treasures that you learn to make, and I hope these slippers will add beauty and comfort to your lives—as they already have to mine.

PART ONE:

MATERIALS AND BASIC TECHNIQUES

Removing my shoes for the day and putting on a pair of cozy slippers is a signal to relax and slow down. Slippers lend themselves to puttering, making an extra pot of coffee, or reading a few more pages of a favorite novel. I delight in having a beautifully embellished pair of slippers to wear everyday, whether lounging around in my yoga pants or getting ready for a dress up event for which I will ultimately put on heels. Slippers are a relatively small knitting project, so it's not difficult to make a pair for everyone in the family.

CHOOSING A STYLE

When you are beginning a new pair of slippers, consider how they will be worn. Slippers you or your kids would wear lounging in bed with the crossword puzzle might be different than ones you wear when stepping outside to gather more firewood. Do you want something super warm and fluffy or something more shoe-like and trim? Do you want your slippers loud and fun or subdued and subtle? You have the opportunity to custom-design slippers so they are just right for the wearer.

CHOOSING YARN

Many of the projects in this book are worked with wool yarn and then felted. Felt is an excellent material for slippers because it is warm and breathable, firm yet flexible. For a project to felt well, I like to use a yarn that is at least 85% wool. Yarn that is machine washable or "superwash" will not felt. A yarn's color can also affect how it will felt. Light colors have typically been bleached, and that changes the structure of the wool and its ability to felt.

When in doubt, try a test swatch. To do this, knit a swatch about 6" (15 cm) square, using the knitting needles called for in the pattern. Check for gauge and then felt well by hand, following the directions on page 14. Did the piece go through all the stages of felting and end up sturdy, firm, and with little stitch definition? If so, the yarn will probably work just fine for your project. If not, you should switch to something else. When choosing yarn for slippers that are not felted, use the yarn called for in the pattern or one with a similar fiber content and structure to ensure the best fit.

GAUGE FOR FELTING

Pieces to be felted are knit at a loose gauge; the patterns in this book call for knitting needles about two sizes larger than the size recommended on the yarn's label. Knitting to gauge is the best way to ensure that your finished slippers will be the correct size. However, there is a bit of flexibility, as you have the opportunity to customize the finished size throughout the felting process.

Clockwise from top to left: Woolly Wellies (page 33), Options Flats (page 99), Rustic Ballet Slippers (page 53), and Lace-Up Boots (page 65).

SIZING AND FIT

Making a pair of slippers for yourself or someone in your immediate family is usually easy because you can try them on during the knitting or felting process and check for fit. Otherwise, use the chart at right and the sizing in the individual patterns to determine what size to make, then work the slippers to the finished dimensions listed in the individual patterns. Felting lends flexibility to sizing: You can felt slippers down to a perfect fit, and if you go a little too far, the slippers can usually be stretched into shape.

	Age or Shoe Size	Foot Circum-ference	Foot Length
Child's XS	2-4 years	6" (15 cm)	6" (15 cm)
Child's S	5-7 years	6½" (16.5 cm)	7" (18 cm)
Child's M	7-9 years	7" (18 cm)	8" (20.5 cm)
Child's L/ Women's S	9-12 years; shoe size women's 4-6	7" (18 cm)	9" (23 cm)
Women's M/ Men's S	Shoe size women's 7-9, men's 6-8	8" (20.5 cm)	10" (25.5 cm)
Women's L/ Men's M	Shoe size women's 10-12, men's 8-11	9" (23 cm)	11" (28 cm)
Men's L	Shoe size men's 11-13	10" (25.5 cm)	12" (30.5 cm)

FELTING

Felting is the process by which wool fibers are changed using heat and friction. Scales on the wool fibers lock together to form something wholly different and new. Applying this process to fiber that has already been knitted or woven was originally called fulling, but now "felting" is a commonly used term for shrinking your knitting. Once you felt something, it cannot be "un-felted"; it's a permanent change. Because felted knits shrink a lot—as much as 60% lengthwise and up to 30% widthwise–your finished slippers will be dense and draft-proof.

When I'm felting, I aim to remove all or most signs of stitch definition. The slippers in this book are designed with that in mind. If you only felt until the piece gets fuzzy, the slippers will be too big and the proportions will be wrong. It's best to felt both slippers at the same time, so that you can make sure they are the same size and shape.

FELTING BY HAND

For all but the largest felting projects, I find it easiest to felt in a dishpan or bowl in the kitchen sink. To begin, add a small squirt of dish soap to the dishpan and fill it half full with really hot water. Put the two matching slippers in the water and let them soak until the water is cool enough to work in. Let one slipper soak in the hot water while working with the other one out of the water, alternating between the two. I frequently dip the piece I'm handling into the hot water, but a lot of my work happens out of the water.

Roll and squeeze the fabric in your hands, or knead it like a small piece of bread dough [1]. I tightly roll and press the piece in my hands, like I'm making a small ball of clay, or rub two sides of a piece against each other.

Roll back and forth between your hands, changing the position of the material often so it felts evenly. If there is a section that is not felting well, let the rest of the piece hang down while working the stubborn bit. Pay attention to the edges; they tend to felt at a slower rate, and it's important that they felt well so the slipper is sturdy and fits properly. I turn the piece inside out and then back again several times, as this allows the surface of the slipper to felt thoroughly and smoothly.

Continue felting until the stitches disappear. To hasten the process, you can add more hot water, squirt a bit of soap directly on the slipper, or dip the piece in cold water–or all three. Try different techniques and see what works for you.

There are several stages a piece goes through when felting:

» First, the material stretches out and expands in the water. It's loose and sometimes difficult to keep it all in your hands.

» Next the stitches start to come together but there is still stitch definition and floppiness. You can tell felting has begun and the piece is growing smaller.

» When the material begins to firm up but still isn't quite there [2], I often hold it to the light to see if I can still see lots of stitch definition. If so, I keep going. Another way to check progress is to measure the piece. Is it the size you want? If not, continue felting This stage seems to last a while and it's easy to quit here. But if you stop now, you may not be pleased with your finished slippers. If you are tired, let the slippers soak in the warm water and take a break. When you return, add new hot water and begin again. If you notice a small hole in the fabric, repair it as shown on page 16.

» Finally, the material is sturdy and firm. The slipper seems to be a different material altogether. The piece will feel noticeably thicker and will stand up on its own [3]. If the slipper is at this stage and not quite the correct size yet, continue to work it to the desired dimensions.

When you are done felting, rinse the slippers in really cold water. This helps to further firm up the piece and removes any extra soap.

Next, roll the felted piece in a towel. Press firmly, to remove as much water as possible [4]. You'll remove any creases in the next step (see page 17).

- { FELTING BY HAND } -

[1] To start, roll and squeeze the fabric in your hands, or knead it like a small piece of bread dough.

[2] Here fabric is firming up but not completely felted yet. Notice how floppy the fabric looks.

[3] After felting is complete, the slipper will be thicker and able to hold itself up.

[4] Roll the felted piece in a towel to remove excess water.

[1] Small holes can appear in the slipper while felting.

[2] Make a small stitch over the top of the hole, beginning and ending on inside of slipper.

[3] Make a second stitch perpendicular to the first.

Sometimes small holes can form on the slipper while you're felting [1]. If you repair them early in the process, you won't be able to see your repair when the piece is fully felted.

To repair holes while felting:
Using a yarn needle threaded with your project yarn, make a small stitch over the top of the hole beginning and ending on the inside of the slipper. Leave a tail about 4" (10 cm) long at the starting point [2].

Leave the yarn loose; don't pull tightly. Make a second stitch perpendicular to the first, then cut, leaving a 4" (10 cm) tail [3]. Securely knot the two tails on the inside of slipper, then cut the tail.

FELTING IN A TOP-LOADING WASHING MACHINE

For larger projects, like the boots in this book, you may find it easier to felt in a top-loading washing machine. You lose some control in the felting process and sometimes pieces turn out less dense, but it is a labor-saving way to felt larger pieces.

To felt in the washing machine, place the slippers in the machine along with a pair or two of jeans. Don't use towels; if you do, lots of lint will be transferred to the slippers and it will be difficult to remove.

Set the machine to its lowest water level, its longest agitation cycle, and to "hot wash/cold rinse." If your water heater is turned down for energy efficiency, add a kettle of boiling water to the machine while it's filling, to speed up felting.

I do not put my child- and adult-sized slippers in a mesh bag. I find they felt better when they are loose in the water, and I have not had trouble with excess fuzz

clogging up the machine. If you are concerned about this, place your items in a lingerie bag. Also, if you are felting very small projects (such as baby booties), you will need to put them in a mesh bag so they don't get stuck in the machine's agitator.

Add a couple tablespoons of laundry detergent and begin the wash cycle. I check the slippers' progress after 5–7 minutes. To help the surface felt evenly, turn the pieces inside out after checking once, then turn them back the next time. When the pieces are getting close to finished, stay near the machine and check progress frequently. One of the downsides to using the washing machine is the risk that the pieces will over-felt and become too small. (See steps in Felting By Hand on pages 14–15 to determine stages of felting.)

When you remove the slippers from the machine, they might look fuzzy and misshapen. Follow the steps on page 17 for shaping, blocking, and shaving.

{ SHAPING AND BLOCKING }

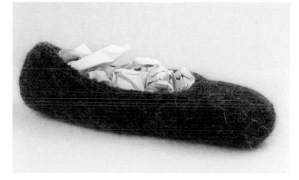

Using newsprint, stuff the slipper smoothly and firmly to shape.

Shaping and blocking may be the most important step in the felting process. This is your opportunity to make the slipper look just right. Wool is very malleable when it is wet, and will hold the shape you have given it when dry. Using newsprint (unprinted if you are working with light-colored wool), stuff the piece smoothly and firmly to shape. Try to make the pair match in size and shaping.

Allow to dry thoroughly. I put my slippers in front of the woodstove or next to a heater vent to hasten drying. Usually they need to dry overnight.

{ SHAVING }

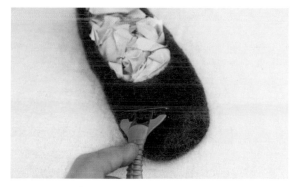

Remove fuzz with a disposable razor.

Different yarns felt differently, but often pieces become very fuzzy after felting. Sometimes the fuzz is a nice feature, but sometimes it becomes tangled and messy-looking. Yarns made with mohair form lots of fuzz. You can easily remove the fuzz with a disposable razor. Shave the piece, stopping occasionally to run the razor backward on a towel to remove the fuzz from the razor.

If necessary, trim any fuzz on the edges of the slippers with a sharp pair of scissors.

SOLING

Slippers with soles are more durable and less slippery than those without soles and they can be worn outside for tasks like checking the mail or watering the garden. I have used several soling options for the projects in this book, and they all have different methods of application. When making your slippers, use the sole that best meets your needs.

{ SOLING WITH PAINT-ON LATEX }

Paint-on latex is the easiest and simplest material for nonslip soling. It is natural latex that goes on milky but dries translucent. I use Castin Craft Mold Builder, which is easy to find at craft stores. This is a good choice if the slippers will only be worn indoors and will not get heavy wear.

To apply, use a disposable foam brush to dab around the perimeter of the sole, then fill in the middle [1]. Don't apply it too thickly; 2 thin coats are best.

Allow to dry, then apply 1 one more coat [2]. If you're in a hurry for the latex to dry, you can heat it with a blow-dryer.

[1] Dab the material around the perimeter of the sole shape, and then fill in the middle.

[2] After the first coat is dry, apply a second coat.

{ SOLING WITH PLASTI DIP }

Plasti Dip is more firm and durable than latex. You can find it in the spray-paint section at the hardware store. When you paint on several coats, it forms a sturdy yet flexible sole. It comes in several primary colors, as well as black and clear. Apply in a well-ventilated space using a disposable foam brush. Outline the perimeter of the sole using short, dabbing strokes, then work toward the center [1].

Don't worry about covering all the wool fiber on the first coat, just focus on making a neat edge.

Set aside to dry. Wrap your brush in plastic wrap to prevent it from drying out. Add 2 more coats of Plasti Dip, allowing it to dry thoroughly between coats [2].

[1] Using a disposable foam brush, dab Plasti Dip around perimeter, then toward the middle.

[2] In total, you will apply three thin coats, allowing each coat to dry between applications.

Suede is easy to sew on. Either recycle leather or suede thrift-store finds (skirts provide big panels of material without seams) or buy suede from a leather crafting shop or fabric store. If you have a leather punch, punch holes around the edge; then sewing on the sole is easy. Or you can skip punching holes and use a leather needle, which has an extra-sharp, angled head that pierces the leather.

To add a full suede sole, trace around your finished slippers onto a piece of paper. Draw a line about ¼" (.5 cm) inside the traced line—this is your cutting line [1]. Cut out the sole template.

Using the paper template as a guide, cut out the suede sole [2]. Be sure to flip the template so you have a right and a left. For a partial sole, copy the template from page 71 and cut it out. If you are punching holes in the suede, lightly mark a line about ¼" (.5 cm) from the edge on the wrong side of the suede and punch holes on this line about ¼" (.5 cm) apart [3].

Secure the suede to the slipper using double-sided or masking tape. Using a regular needle (or a leather needle, if you haven't punched holes) and embroidery floss that matches the slipper, sew it to the sole [4].

[1] To make a paper template for sole, trace around finished slipper and then ¼" (.5 cm) in from traced line (inside line is cutting line).

[2] Use paper template and scissors to cut out suede sole.

[3] Mark holes about ¼" (.5 cm) apart, about ¼" (.5 cm) in from edge of sole, then punch out.

[4] Sew sole to slipper with embroidery floss.

{ VEGETABLE-TANNED LEATHER SOLING }

Firm vegetable-tanned leather is a good soling choice if you'd like a natural material that is very durable. Using this as a sole will make a slipper that is almost as firm and sturdy as a shoe. I use 5–6 oz. leather that is available from a leather crafting store. Vegetable-tanned leather is thick and sometimes difficult to work with, so use a sharp utility knife when cutting it out. Trace around your finished slippers onto a piece of paper [1]. Draw a line about ¼" (.5 cm) inside the traced line—this is your cutting line. Transfer the pattern to the leather,

making sure to flip the template so you have a right and a left [2]. Cut out the soles with a utility knife. Lightly mark a line about ¼" (.5 cm) from the edge on the wrong (fuzzy) side of the leather and use a leather punch to create holes on this line about ¼" (.5 cm) apart [3]. Secure the leather to the slipper using double-sided or masking tape. Using a large-eyed sewing needle and well-waxed embroidery floss, sew the sole to the slipper [4].

[1] To make a paper template for sole, trace around finished slipper and then ¼" (.5 cm) in from traced line (inside line is cutting line).

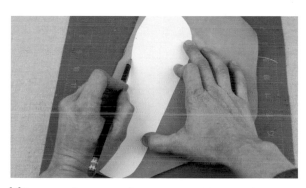

[2] Turn around paper template onto vegetable-tanned leather sole.

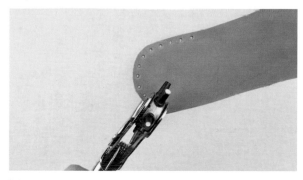

[3] Mark holes about ¼" (.5 cm) apart and about ¼" (.5 cm) in from edge of sole, then punch out.

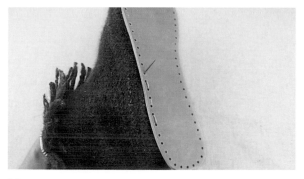

[4] Sew sole to slipper with embroidery floss.

LINING

Lining adds cushioning and warmth, makes slippers more durable, and contributes structure and body. Some slippers, like those knit with two strands of yarn, are already very cozy and sturdy and don't require a lining. Some trim slippers, like the Beaded Moccs (page 81), were designed with a lining in mind, so the fit will be a bit big if you choose not to make a lining.

{ SHEARLING LINING }

Shearling lining is cozy and wears well. You can buy shearling at leather crafting stores or you can buy a small, inexpensive sheepskin rug from places like IKEA. From one small sheepskin, you will have enough shearling for several pairs of slippers.

To make a template for the shearling lining, trace around the bottom of the finished slipper on a piece of paper [1]. Draw a line about ¼" (.5 cm) in from the traced line—this is your cutting line. Cut out the lining template. Place the template on the back of the shearling, trace it, and cut it out [2]. Flip the template over, trace, and cut out a second piece. To trim shearling, cut off tips of wool using smooth, even cuts. Put glue on the back of the shearling and glue in place inside the slipper. Use E600 craft glue if you are planning to wash the piece in the washing machine, or Aileen's tacky glue if you are not.

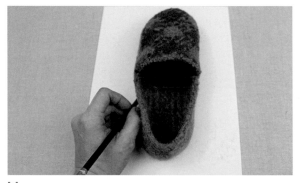

[1] Place template on cutting lining, trace, and cut out.

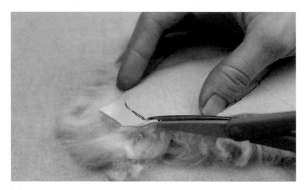

[2] Trace and cut out shearling pieces.

-------------------- { SEWN LINING AND LINING CORE } --------------------

When making linings from recycled wool sweaters or wool felt, I always use two layers of fabric. For stability and comfort I sometimes add an inner core that I make out of thin foam, cushy felted wool, or fleece. To make the lining pieces, first trace around the bottom of the finished slipper onto a piece of paper. Iron your lining fabric and fold it, with right sides together. Place the template on the folded piece of lining material, trace it, and cut out the two linings [1].

Flip your template and cut out another pair. Pin the matching pieces together and machine- or hand-sew securely, using a ¼" (.5 cm) seam allowance. Leave a 2" (5 cm) opening to turn. Clip curves [2] and turn right-side out. If you want to make a lining core, use the sewn lining as a template to cut out one core for each slipper. Carefully insert the core into the lining [3], then sew the opening closed. Add topstitching to secure the layers together [4].

[1] Place template on folded lining fabric, trace, and cut out.

[2] Sew together two lining layers, leaving 2" (.5 cm) opening, then clip curves, and turn right-side out.

[3] Insert core into lining.

[4] Sew opening closed and topstitch to secure layers.

SLIPPER CARE AND REPAIR

WASHING

Happily, wool is naturally antimicrobial and breathable, so wool slippers do not require frequent laundering. It's easy to spot clean your slippers. Wipe with a damp rag or gently scrub with a soft brush. Blot excess water with a dry rag. For more intense cleaning, if you did not glue down the lining, remove the lining and wash the slipper in a cold, delicate cycle in the washing machine. (If you glued down the lining with E600 craft glue, you may wash the slippers with the lining left in.) Remove from the washing machine promptly, shape well by stuffing with newsprint again, and allow to dry.

FIXING HOLES

Holes can appear in the toe and heel areas of slippers, particularly those that don't have a sole. To repair, stitch over the hole as explained on page 16, working several stitches in one direction and several stitches perpendicular. To ensure that the repair holds up, pack your stitches in tightly. Alternately, you can pull matching wool yarn apart to make loose "roving" and needle felt (see page 151) a covering into place. If you're using thin yarn, you'll have to needle felt several layers for this to work.

CORRECTING SIZING

After a lot of wear, slippers may stretch out a bit. You can re-felt them by washing them in the machine on a hot wash cycle, checking partway through to ensure they don't felt too much.

PROJECTS

- FIRESIDE BOOTIES -

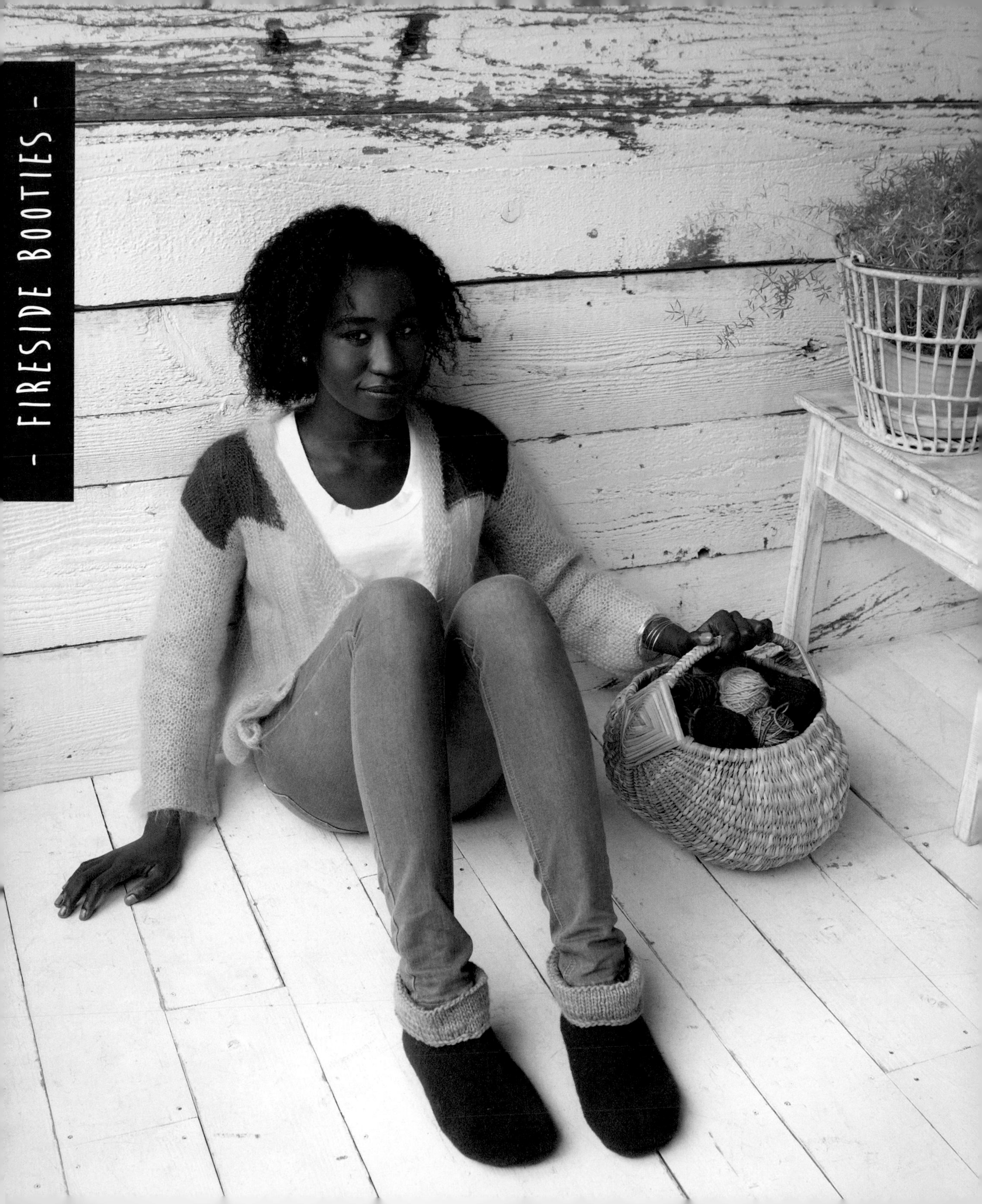

These bright slippers warm both the feet and the ankles. The foot portion is sewn with either fabric from a felted wool sweater or purchased boiled wool. The contrasting knitted cuff is then sewn on. These booties are easy to complete in a night and can be made in either child or adult sizes.

SIZES
Child's X-Small (Child's Small, Child's Medium, Child's Large/Women's Small, Women's Medium/Men's Small, Women's Large/Men's Medium, Men's Large)

FINISHED MEASUREMENTS
6¼ (7¼, 8½, 9½, 10½, 11½, 12½)" [16 (18.5, 21.5, 24, 26.5, 29, 32) cm] Foot circumference
6 (7, 8, 9, 10, 11, 12)" [15 (18, 20.5, 23, 25.5, 28, 30.5) cm] Foot length

YARN
Manos del Uruguay Wool Clasica [100% wool; 138 yards (125 meters) / 100 grams]: 1 hank #68 Citric

NEEDLES
One pair straight needles size US 8 (5 mm); change needle size if necessary to obtain correct gauge.

NOTIONS
Adult-size wool sweater or about ½ yard (.5 meter) boiled wool; ½ yard (.5 meter) flannel, fleece, felt, or unfelted wool sweater, for lining; sewing needle or sewing machine and sewing thread; yarn needle

GAUGE
16 sts and 20 rows l 4" (10 cm) in Stockinette stitch (St st)

OVERVIEW

The Body of each Bootie is made from two pieces cut out of a felted sweater or boiled wool, then sewn together. The knitted Cuff is worked back and forth, then the side edges are sewn together and the Cuff is sewn to the Body.

SLIPPER BODY

If necessary, felt sweater in washing machine with 1 or 2 pairs of jeans. Wash in hot wash/cold rinse cycle with just a bit of soap. Remove from washer and tug into shape. Allow to dry flat. If sweater has side seams, cut out seams and discard. If using boiled wool, skip this step.

Photocopy Sole and Upper templates, reducing or enlarging as indicated for your size, and cut out templates. Fold sweater or boiled wool and place dotted line of Upper template on fold line of fabric, making sure to plan ahead so that you have enough fabric to cut out 2 Sole pieces as well. Cut out 1 Upper, cutting through both layers; do not cut along fold line. Cut out 2 Soles using template [1].

With RSs of Upper together, using sewing machine or needle and sewing thread and ¼" (.5 cm) seam allowance, sew heel seam. With WSs of pieces facing, pin Upper to Sole at center back and center front of each piece, then halfway along each side. Continue to pin Upper to Sole, easing Upper to fit evenly around Sole.

Using ¼" (.5 cm) seam allowance, sew Upper to Sole. Trim seams close to stitching [2].

Turn Slipper Body RS out. Set aside [3].

CUFF

CO 34 (34, 42, 46, 50, 57, 61) sts. Begin St st, beginning with a purl row; work even for 8 (8, 8, 10, 10, 12, 12) rows. Knit 1 row (Turning Row). Work even in St st for 7 (7, 7, 9, 9, 11, 11) rows. BO all sts.

FINISHING

Using working yarn and yarn needle, sew side edges of Cuff together. Fold in half lengthwise; sew CO and BO edges together. Pin Cuff to Slipper Body, so Cuff edge overlaps Body by about ½" (1.5 cm). Sew Cuff to Body, using bars between knit sts to ensure seam sts are invisible [4].

Lining and Soling

Add lining (see page 22) and soling (see page 18) of your choice. I used a recycled-wool lining and sewn-on suede soling.

-- { MAKING SLIPPER BODY } --

[1] Cut out Sole and Upper pieces using template.

[2] Pin Upper to fit evenly around Sole.

[3] Sew seams and trim close to stitching.

-- { ADDING KNITTED CUFF } --

[4] Sew Cuff to Body with working yarn.

--- { FIRESIDE BOOTIES TEMPLATE } ---

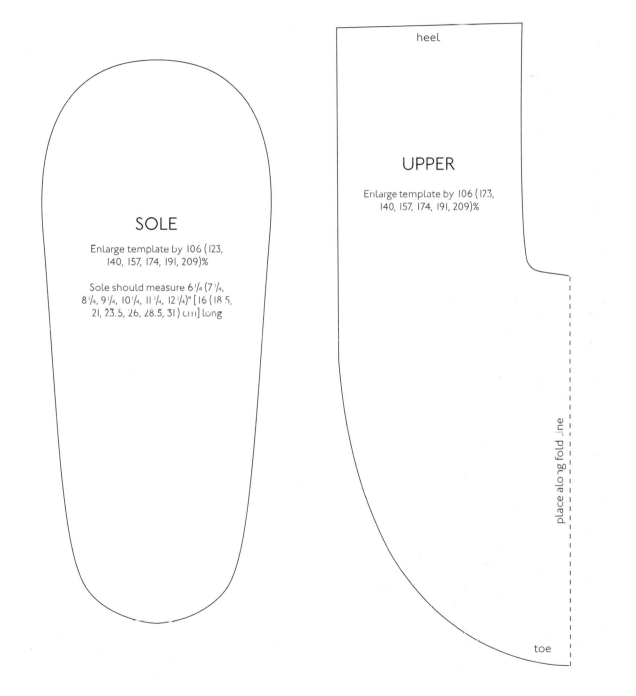

heel

UPPER

Enlarge template by 106 (123, 140, 157, 174, 191, 209)%

SOLE

Enlarge template by 106 (123, 140, 157, 174, 191, 209)%

Sole should measure 6 1/4 (7 1/4, 8 1/4, 9 1/4, 10 1/4, 11 1/4, 12 1/4)" [16 (18.5, 21, 23.5, 26, 28.5, 31) cm] long

place along fold line

toe

These are my woolly take on the classic waterproof rubber boots called Wellingtons (or Wellies, for short). A knitted (but not felted) inner cuff in a contrasting color lines the leg portion for extra coziness in these unisex slippers.

SIZES
Women's Small (Women's Medium/Men's Small, Women's Large/Men's Medium, Men's Large)

FINISHED MEASUREMENTS
11 1/2 (13, 13 3/4, 15)" [29 (33, 35, 37) cm] Foot circumference, before felting
9 1/2 (11, 11, 12 1/2)" [24 (28, 28, 32) cm] inside Foot circumference, after felting
11 (12 1/4, 13 3/4, 14 3/4)" [28 (31, 35, 37.5) cm] Foot length, before felting
9, (10, 11, 12)" [23 (25.5, 28, 30.5) cm] Foot length, after felting

YARN
Brown Sheep Lamb's Pride Worsted [85% wool / 15% mohair; 190 yards (174 meters) / 4 ounces (114 grams)]: 2 (2, 3, 3) skeins #M113 Oregano (MC)

Malabrigo Merino Worsted [100% wool; 210 yards (192 meters) / 100 grams]: 1 hank #135 Emerald (A)

NEEDLES
One set of five double-pointed needles (dpn) size US 13 (9 mm); one set of five double-pointed needles size US 4 (3.5 mm); change needle size if necessary to obtain correct gauge

NOTIONS
Stitch marker; non-felting waste yarn; disposable razor

GAUGE
10 1/2 sts and 12 rows = 4" (10 cm) in Stockinette stitch (St st), using larger needles and 2 strands of MC held together
24 sts and 32 rows = 4" (10 cm) in 3x1 Rib, using smaller needles and 1 strand of A

OVERVIEW

The Leg is worked back and forth, then additional stitches are cast on for the Foot and the piece is joined to work in the round. The Heel is shaped using short rows, then the Foot and shaped Toe are worked in the round. The Ribbed Cuff Lining is worked in the round, then the Boots (not including the Cuff Lining) are felted. The Boot is turned inside out and the Cuff Lining is sewn to the wrong side of the Boot.

STITCH PATTERN

3x1 Rib

(multiple of 4 sts; 1-rnd repeat)
All Rnds: *K3, p1; repeat from * to end.

LEFT BOOT
LEG

Using larger needles and 2 strands of MC held together, CO 32 (36, 36, 40) sts. Begin St st, beginning with a purl row; work even for 10 (12, 14, 16) rows, slipping the first st of every row.

End Slit

Next Row (RS): Using Backward Loop CO (see Special Techniques, page 151), CO 4 sts, knit to end—36 (40, 40, 44) sts. Join for working in the rnd; pm for beginning of rnd.
Next Rnd: *K7 (8, 8, 9), k2tog; repeat from * to end—32 (36, 36, 40) sts remain.

HEEL FLAP

Row 1 (RS): K3, pm, k16 (18, 18, 20), turn.
Row 2 (WS): P16 (18, 18, 20), turn.
Repeat Rows 1 and 2 two (3, 3, 4) times, then Row 1 once.

HEEL

Note: Heel is shaped using short rows (see Special Techniques, page 152); work wraps together with wrapped sts as you come to them.
Short Row 1 (RS): K9 (11, 11, 13), k2tog, wrp-t— 15 (17, 17, 19) sts remain.
Short Row 2: P3 (5, 5, 7), p2tog, wrp-t— 14 (16, 16, 18) sts remain.
Short Row 3: K4 (6, 6, 8), k2tog, wrp-t— 13 (15, 15, 17) sts remain.
Short Row 4: P5 (7, 7, 9), p2tog, wrp-t— 12 (14, 14, 16) sts remain.

Short Row 5: K6 (8, 8, 10), k2tog, wrp-t— 11 (13, 13, 15) sts remain.
Short Row 6: P7 (9, 9, 11), p2tog, wrp-t— 10 (12, 12, 14) sts remain.

FOOT

Next Row (RS): K5 (6, 6, 7). Join for working in the rnd; pm for beginning of rnd, K5 (6, 6, 7) pick up and knit 6 (7, 7, 8) sts from edge of Heel Flap, k16 (18, 18, 20), pick up and knit 6 (7, 7, 8) sts from edge of Heel Flap, k5 (6, 6, 7)—38 (44, 44, 50) sts. Knit 1 rnd. Place markers 12 (14, 14, 16) sts to either side of beginning-of-rnd marker.
Decrease Rnd 1: Decrease 2 sts this rnd, then every other rnd 3 times, as follows: Knit to 2 sts before marker, k2tog, sm, knit to next marker, sm, k2tog, knit to end— 30 (36, 36, 42) sts remain. Knit 0 (1, 0, 1) rnd(s).

SIZES WOMEN'S MEDIUM/MEN'S SMALL AND MEN'S LARGE ONLY

Decrease Rnd 2: K- (8, -, 10), k2tog, k- (16, -, 18), k2tog, k- (8, -, 10)—- (34, -, 40) sts remain.

SIZE MEN'S LARGE ONLY

Knit 1 rnd.
Decrease Rnd 3: K9, k2tog, k18, k2tog, k9—38 sts remain.

ALL SIZES

Knit 14 (14, 20, 18) rnds.

TOE
SIZES WOMEN'S SMALL, WOMEN'S MEDIUM/MEN'S SMALL, AND MEN'S LARGE ONLY

Decrease Rnd 1: K7 (8, -, 9), k2tog, k13 (15, -, 17), k2tog, k6 (7, - 8)—28 (32, -, 36) sts remain.

SIZES WOMEN'S LARGE/MEN'S MEDIUM ONLY

Decrease Rnd 2: *K7, k2tog; repeat from * to end—32 sts remain.

ALL SIZES

Decrease Rnd 3: *K5 (6, 6, 7), k2tog; repeat from * to end—24 (28, 28, 32) sts remain. Knit 1 rnd.

Decrease Rnd 4: *K4 (5, 5, 6), k2tog; repeat from * to end—20 (24, 24, 28) sts remain. Knit 1 rnd.

Decrease Rnd 5: *K3 (4, 4, 5), k2tog; repeat from * to end—16 (20, 20, 24) sts remain. Knit 1 rnd.

Decrease Rnd 6: *K2 (3, 3, 4), k2tog; repeat from * to end—12 (16, 16, 20) sts remain. Knit 1 rnd.

Decrease Rnd 7: *K1 (2, 2, 3), k2tog; repeat from * to end—8 (12, 12, 16) sts remain. Knit 0 (1, 1, 1) rnd(s).

SIZES WOMEN'S MEDIUM/MEN'S SMALL, WOMEN'S LARGE/MEN'S MEDIUM, AND MEN'S LARGE ONLY

Decrease Rnd 8: *K– (1, 1, 2), k2tog; repeat from * to end—– (8, 8, 12) sts remain.

SIZE MEN'S LARGE ONLY

Decrease Rnd 9: *K1, k2tog; repeat from * to end—8 sts remain.

ALL SIZES

Cut yarn, leaving an 8" (20.5 cm) tail. Thread tail through remaining sts, pull tight, and fasten off.

RIGHT BOOT

Work as for Left Boot to beginning of Heel Flap.

Row 1 (RS): K17 (19, 19, 21), pm, k16 (18, 18, 20) (1 st past beginning-of-rnd marker), turn.

Row 2 (WS): P16 (18, 18, 20), turn.

Repeat Rows 1 and 2 two (3, 3, 4) times, then Row 1 once. Complete as for Left Boot.

RIBBED CUFF LINING

Using smaller needles and 1 strand of A, loosely CO 68 (72, 72, 80) sts. Join for working in the rnd, being careful not to twist sts; pm for beginning of rnd. Begin 3x1 Rib; work even until piece measures 4 1/2 (5, 5 1/2, 6)" [11 (12.5, 14, 15) cm]. BO all sts loosely knitwise.

FINISHING

Felting

Using non-felting waste yarn, sew a zigzag between open side edges of Leg, keeping sts long and knotting each st as you sew it, so that sides hold their shape when felting; do not sew side edges closed [1]. Felt Boots well (see page 14). While piece is still damp, stuff with newsprint to shape. Round toe into a pleasing shape and tug Sole to finished length [2]. To remove excess fuzz, shave piece with a disposable razor. Allow to dry thoroughly. Remove waste yarn. Turn Boot inside out and sew CO edge of Ribbed Cuff Lining to WS of Boot, below base of Leg slit, using small sts and being careful not to let sts show on RS of Boot [3].

- - - - - - - - - - - - - - - - - - { BEFORE AND AFTER FELTING } - - - - - - - - - - - - - - - - - -

[1] Before felting, so Leg holds its shape, use non-felting waste yarn to sew a zigzag between open side edges of Leg.

[2] After felting, while Boots are still damp, stuff with newsprint, round Toe, and tug Sole to finished length.

[3] Sew CO edge of ribbed Cuff Lining to WS of Boot, below base of leg slit.

Here a fox and rabbit find sleepy harmony on little feet. The ultimate in cute, and a definite crowd-pleaser!

SIZES
Child's X-Small (Small, Medium, Large)

FINISHED MEASUREMENTS
6 (7, 8, 9)" [15 (18, 20.5, 23) cm] long

YARN
Spud & Chloë Outer [65% wool / 35% organic cotton; 60 yards (55 meters) / 100 grams]: 1 hank each #7209 Cedar (A) and #7212 Sandbox (B)

NEEDLES
One set of five double-pointed needles (dpn) size US 10½ (6.5 mm); change needle size if necessary to obtain correct gauge

NOTIONS
Embroidery floss in pink, black, and brown; embroidery needle

GAUGE
12 sts and 16 rows = 4" (10 cm) in Stockinette stitch (St st)

OVERVIEW
The Foot is worked back and forth to the end of the Foot opening, then stitches are cast on and the Foot is worked in the round, finishing with a simple shaped Toe. The Tails and Ears are worked separately, then sewn to the Slippers.

FOX

Foot

Using A, CO 16 (18, 20, 20) sts. Begin St st, beginning with a purl row; work even for 11 (13, 15, 17) rows, slipping the first st of every row.

Next Row (RS): Knit to end; using Backward Loop CO (see Special Techniques, page 151), CO 2 (3, 4, 4) sts. Join for working in the round; pm for beginning of rnd—18 (21, 24, 24) sts. Knit 8 (10, 12, 14) rnds.

Toe

Shape Toe

Decrease Rnd 1: *K1, k2tog; repeat from * to end—12 (14, 16, 16) sts remain. Knit 1 rnd.

Decrease Rnd 2: *K2tog; repeat from * to end—6 (7, 8, 8) sts remain.** Knit 1 rnd.

Decrease Rnd 3: K2tog, k0 (1, 1, 1), k2tog, k0 (0, 1, 1), k2tog—3 (4, 5, 5) sts remain. Cut yarn, leaving a 6" (15 cm) tail; thread through remaining sts, pull tight, and fasten off.

Tail

Using A, CO 9 sts. Join for working in the rnd, being careful not to twist sts; pm for beginning of rnd. Knit 9 rnds.

Next Rnd: Change to B. [K1, k2tog] 3 times—6 sts remain. Knit 2 rnds.

Next Rnd: [K2tog] 3 times—3 sts remain. Cut yarn, leaving a 6" (15 cm) tail; thread through remaining sts, pull tight, and fasten off.

Ears

Using A, CO 3 sts. Purl 1 row. Knit 1 row.

Next Row: P3tog—1 st remains. Knit 1 row. Fasten off.

Finishing

Fold CO edge of Foot in half and sew edges together for back seam. Sew Ears to head and Tail to back seam [1]. Using black embroidery floss and embroidery needle, sew 6–7 straight sts across tip of Toe for nose. Using brown embroidery floss, sew 4–5 straight sts across 1 knit st for each eye.

---- { ATTACH EARS AND TAIL TO FOX } ----

[1] Sew Ears to head and Tail to back seam.

RABBIT

Using B, work as for Fox through ** at end of Toe Decrease Rnd 2—6 (7, 8, 8) sts remain. Cut yarn, leaving a 6" (15 cm) tail; thread through remaining sts, pull tight, and fasten off.

Pom-Pom Tail

Using B, wrap yarn 40 times around 4 fingers. Carefully remove loops from hand and tie loops together tightly in middle using additional 6" (15 cm) long strand. Cut loop ends and trim to make a full pom-pom.

Ears

Using B, CO 3 sts. Begin St st, beginning with a purl row; work even for 6 rows.
Next Row: P3tog—1 st remains. Knit 1 row. Fasten off.

Finishing

Fold CO edge of Foot in half and sew edges together for back seam. Sew Ears to head and Tail to back seam [1]. Using pink embroidery floss and embroidery needle, sew 6—7 straight sts across 2 knit sts at tip of Toe for nose [2]. Using brown embroidery floss, sew 4—5 straight sts for eyes across 1 knit st for each eye

{ EMBROIDER NOSE ON RABBIT }

[2] Using pink embroidery floss and embroidery needle, sew 6—7 straight sts across 2 knit sts at tip of Toe for nose.

A cluster of miniature pom-poms enlivens these comfortable seed-stitch flats. Have fun using up some of your stash yarn to make these simple, colorful embellishments.

SIZES
Women's Small (Medium, Large)

FINISHED MEASUREMENTS
$8^{3}/_{4}$ ($9^{3}/_{4}$, $10^{3}/_{4}$)" [22 (25.5, 27) cm] Foot length
Note: Flats are intended to be worn with approximately $^{1}/_{4}$" (.5 cm) negative ease.

YARN
Rowan Purelife British Sheep Breeds Chunky Undyed [100% British wool; 120 yards (110 meters) / 100 grams]:
1 skein #955 Shetland Moorit
Approximately 5 yards (4.5 meters) each of 6 yarns in worsted, DK, or fingering weight, for Pom-Poms

NEEDLES
One set of five double-pointed needles (dpn) size US 8 (5 mm); change needle size if necessary to obtain correct gauge

NOTIONS
Stitch marker; fork; tapestry needle; sewing needle and thread

GAUGE
15 sts and 25 rows = 4" (10 cm) in Seed stitch

OVERVIEW
The Foot is worked back and forth to the end of the Foot opening; then stitches are cast on for the Toe, and the Toe is worked in the round, finishing with simple shaping.

STITCH PATTERNS

Seed Stitch Flat
(multiple of 2 sts; 1-row repeat)
All Rows: K1, *p1, k1; repeat from * to end.

Seed Stitch in the Rnd
Rnd 1: P1, *k1, p1; repeat from * to end.
Rnd 2: K1, *p1, k1; repeat from * to end.
Repeat Rnds 1 and 2 for Seed Stitch in the Rnd.

FOOT

CO 21 (23, 25) sts. Begin Seed Stitch Flat and work even until piece measures 5 (5½, 6)" [12.5 (14, 15) cm] from the beginning.
Next Row (RS): Continuing in Seed Stitch Flat and using Backward Loop CO (see Special Techniques, page 151), CO 2 sts at beginning of next 2 rows—25 (27, 29) sts.

TOE

Next Row (RS): Using Backward Loop CO, CO 6 sts, pm for beginning of rnd, work to end. Join for working in the rnd—31 (33, 35) sts. Change to Seed Stitch in Rnds; work even for 9 (11, 15) rnds.

Shape Toe
Decrease Rnd 1: Continuing in Seed Stitch in Rnds, k1, p1, k1, p3tog, work 13 (15, 17) sts, p3tog, work to end—27 (29, 31) sts remain. Work even for 1 rnd.

Decrease Rnd 2: K1, p1, k3tog, work 11 (13, 15) sts, k3tog, work to end—23 (25, 27) sts remain. Work even for 1 rnd.
Decrease Rnd 3: K1, p3tog, work 9 (11, 13) sts, p3tog, work to end—19 (21, 23) sts remain. Work even for 1 rnd.
Decrease Rnd 4: K3tog, work 7 (9, 11) sts, k3tog, work to end—15 (17, 19) sts remain. Work even for 1 rnd.
Decrease Rnd 4: K3tog, p3tog, [k1, p1] 0 (1, 2) time(s), k3tog, p3tog, k1, p1, k1—7 (9, 11) sts. Cut yarn, leaving a 6" (15 cm) tail; thread through remaining sts, pull tight, and fasten off.

FINISHING

Fold CO edge of Foot in half and sew edges together for heel seam.

Mini Pom-Poms (make 6 in yarns and colors of your choice)
Wrap yarn around fork approximately 40 times [1]. Cut yarn. Cut 1 strand in matching color 1 yard (30 cm) long; thread through tapestry needle. Thread needle through tines of fork and around center of wraps; tie tightly [2]. Remove yarn from fork, then cut yarn at both sides to "release" Pom-Pom [3]. Trim Pom-Pom as desired. Using sewing needle and thread, sew to Slipper [4].

{ MAKING AND APPLYING MINI POM-POMS }

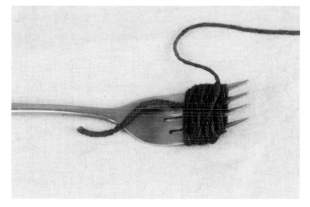

[1] To make Mini Pom-Poms, wrap yarn around fork approximately 40 times, then cut end.

[2] Thread needle with a seperate length of yarn through tines of fork and around center of wraps; tie tightly.

[3] Cut yarn at both sides to "release" Pom-Pom.

[4] Using sewing needle and thread, sew Pom-Poms to Slipper.

Inspired by Renaissance style, these slim-fitting boot slippers can be worn straight up or folded down. The flare at the top is a natural result of the felting process—edges tend to felt less than the rest of a piece. The decorative cord is optional.

SIZES
Women's Small (Medium, Large)

FINISHED MEASUREMENTS
12¼ (13¼, 14¼)" [31 (33.5, 36) cm] Foot length, before felting
9 (10, 11)" [23 (25.5, 28) cm] Foot length, after felting
15½ (17, 17) [39.5 (43, 43) cm] Leg length, before felting
11 (12, 12)" [28 (30.5, 30.5) cm] Leg length, after felting

YARN
Manos del Uruguay Wool Clasica [100% wool; 138 yards (125 meters) / 100 grams]: 3 hanks #44 Briar (MC); 1 hank #40 Goldenrod (A) (optional)
Note: If the yarn you are working with is a semisolid color (like the Manos yarn I used) or a variegated color, you may avoid color pooling by working with 2 balls, alternating 1 row/rnd from each ball. Work the Heel with 1 ball, then go back to alternating rows for the rest of the Boot.

NEEDLES
One set of five double-pointed needles (dpn) size US 10½ (6.5 mm); change needle size if necessary to obtain correct gauge

NOTIONS
Crochet hook size US J/10 (6 mm); stitch marker; newsprint; disposable razor; piece of shearling large enough to accommodate two linings; craft glue; black Plasti Dip rubber coating or soling material of your choice; disposable brush

GAUGE
12 sts and 16 rows = 4" (10 cm) in Stockinette stitch (St st)

OVERVIEW

The Leg is worked in the round, then the Heel is shaped using short rows. The Foot and shaped Toe are worked in the round.

LEG

Using MC, CO 50 (50, 52) sts. Join for working in the rnd, being careful not to twists sts; pm for beginning of rnd. Knit 62 (68, 68) rnds, decreasing 2 (2, 0) sts evenly on last rnd—48 (48, 52) sts remain.

HEEL

Transfer last 12 (12, 13) sts worked to empty needle. You will work Heel across first 13 (13, 14) sts of rnd and last 12 (12, 13) sts of rnd, leaving remaining 23 (23, 25) sts out of work.

Note: Heel will be shaped using short rows (see Special Techniques, page 152); work wraps together with wrapped sts as you come to them.

Short Row 1 (RS): K12 (12, 13), wrp-t.
Short Row 2 (WS): P23 (23, 25), wrp-t.
Short Row 3: K22 (22, 24), wrp-t.
Short Row 4: P21 (21, 23), wrp-t.
Short Row 5: K20 (20, 22), wrp-t.
Short Row 6: P19 (19, 21), wrp-t.
Short Row 7: K18 (18, 20), wrp-t.
Short Row 8: P17 (17, 19), wrp-t.
Short Row 9: K16 (16, 18), wrp-t.
Short Row 10: P15 (15, 17), wrp-t.
Short Row 11: K14 (14, 16), wrp-t.
Short Row 12: P13 (13, 15), wrp-t.
Short Row 13: K12 (12, 14), wrp-t.

SIZE LARGE ONLY

Short Row 14: P13, wrp-t.
Short Row 15: K14, wrp-t.

ALL SIZES

Short Row 16: P13 (13, 15), wrp-t.
Short Row 17: K14 (14, 16), wrp-t.
Short Row 18: P15 (15, 17), wrp-t.
Short Row 19: K16 (16, 18), wrp-t.
Short Row 20: P17 (17, 19), wrp-t.
Short Row 21: K18 (18, 20), wrp-t.
Short Row 22: P19 (19, 21), wrp-t.
Short Row 23: K20 (20, 22), wrp-t.

Short Row 24: P21 (21, 23), wrp-t.
Short Row 25: K22 (22, 24), wrp-t.
Short Row 26: P23 (23, 25), wrp-t.
Short Row 27: K12 (12, 13). Do not turn.

FOOT

Join for working in the rnd; pm for beginning of rnd. Knit 3 rnds.

Decrease Rnd 1: K11 (11, 12), k2tog, k22 (22, 24), k2tog, k11 (11, 12)—46 (46, 50) sts remain. Knit 3 rnds.
Decrease Rnd 2: K10 (10, 11), k2tog, k22 (22, 24), k2tog, k10 (10, 11)—44 (44, 48) sts remain. Knit 3 rnds.
Decrease Rnd 3: K10 (10, 11), k2tog, k20 (20, 22), k2tog, k10 (10, 11)—42 (42, 46) sts remain. Knit 3 rnds.
Decrease Rnd 4: K9 (9, 10), k2tog, k20 (20, 22), k2tog, k9 (9, 10)—40 (40, 44) sts. Knit 5 (9, 12) rnds. Place marker after st 13 (13, 15) for Right Boot; place marker after st 27 (27, 29) for Left Boot.
Decrease Rnd 5: Decrease 2 sts this rnd, then every 3 rnds 3 times, as follows: Knit to 3 sts before marker, k2tog, k1, sm, k1, k2tog, knit to end— 32 (32, 36) sts remain.

TOE

SIZE LARGE ONLY

Decrease Rnd 6: K6, ssk, k2, k2tog, k12, ssk, k2, k2tog, k6—32 sts remain.

ALL SIZES

Decrease Rnd 7: K5, ssk, k2, k2tog, k10, ssk, k2, k2tog, k5—28 sts remain.
Decrease Rnd 8: K4, ssk, k2, k2tog, k8, ssk, k2, k2tog, k4—24 sts remain.
Decrease Rnd 9: K3, ssk, k2, k2tog, k6, ssk, k2, k2tog, k3—20 sts remain.
Decrease Rnd 10: K2, ssk, k2, k2tog, k4, ssk, k2, k2tog, k2— 16 sts remain.
Decrease Rnd 11: K1, ssk, k2, k2tog, k2, ssk, k2, k2tog, k1— 12 sts remain. Cut yarn, leaving an 8" (20.5 cm) tail. Thread tail through remaining sts, pull tight, and fasten off.

{ CREATE WRAP TIES }

[1] About 6" (15 cm) from end of fastened-off crochet chain, work another 6" (15 cm) crochet chain.

[2] Work third crochet chain next to the second, then repeat for opposite end of Tie.

FINISHING

Felt Boots (see page 14). While piece is still damp, stuff with newsprint to shape. Round toe into a pleasing shape and tug Sole to finished length. To remove excess fuzz, shave piece with a disposable razor (see page 17). Allow to dry thoroughly.

Soling and Lining

Add soling (see page 18) and lining (see page 22) of your choice. I lined mine with wool shearling and painted on Plasti Dip soling.

Wrap Ties (make 2)

Using crochet hook and A, work crochet chain for approximately 65" (165 cm). Fasten off. Rejoin yarn to one end of one Tie, 6" (15 cm) from end. Work crochet chain for approximately 6" (15 cm) [1]. Work second crochet chain next to the first, then repeat for opposite end of Tie. Repeat for second Tie [2]. Felt by hand (see page 14), until piece measures approximately 45" [114.5 cm] long. Loosely wrap around Leg of Boot, and tie.

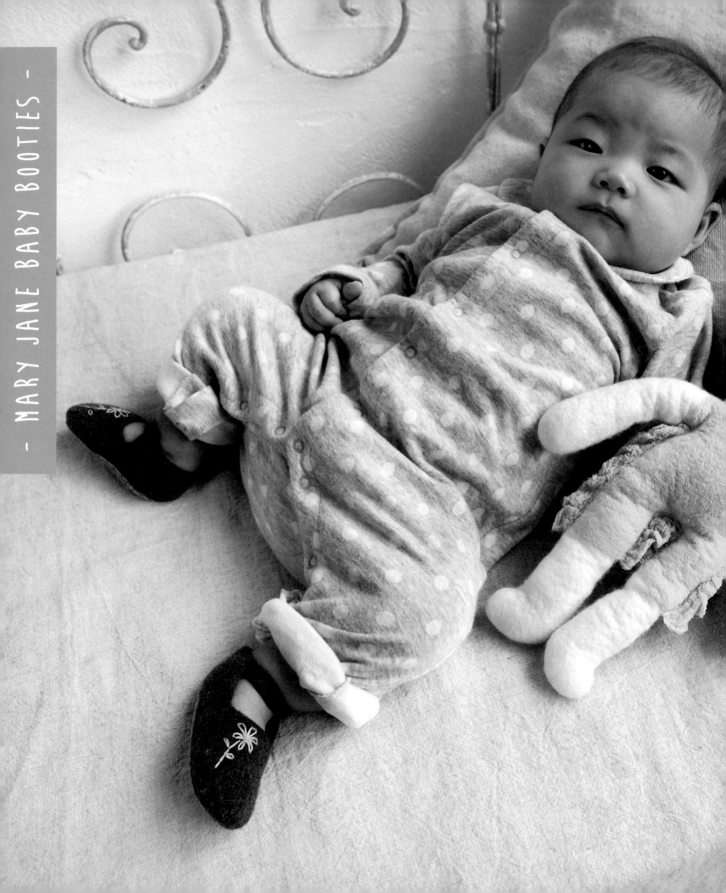

Adorned with pearl buttons and simple embroidery, these sweet booties draw inspiration from the classic Mary Jane style. Worked in fingering weight wool, these booties are thin and supple.

SIZES
3–6 (6–12, 12–18) months

FINISHED MEASUREMENTS
4 (4½, 5)" [10 (11, 12.5) cm] Foot length

YARN
Brooklyn Tweed Loft (100% Targhee-Columbia wool; 275 yards (251 meters) / 50 grams): 1 hank # 13 Wool Socks

NEEDLES
One set of five double-pointed needles (dpn) size US 7 (4.5 mm); change needle size if necessary to obtain correct gauge

NOTIONS
Crochet hook size US H/8 (5 mm) or one size larger; stitch marker; two ¼" (.5 cm) buttons; waxed embroidery floss in pink, yellow, and green; embroidery needle

GAUGE
20 sts and 28 rows = 4" (10 cm) in Stockinette stitch (St st)

OVERVIEW
The Booties are worked from the Toe up, beginning with a provisional cast-on and shaping the Toe using short rows. The Foot is picked up from the provisional cast-on and worked back and forth to the Heel, which is shaped using short rows. An I-Cord Edging is worked around the Foot opening to give structure to the edges. The Strap is picked up from the side of the Heel Flap and worked for several rows. The Booties are felted, then embellished with embroidery.

TOE

Using crochet hook, waste yarn, and Provisional CO (see Special Techniques, page 152), CO 16 (18, 20) sts. Change to working yarn.

Shape Toe

Note: Toe is shaped using short rows (see Special Techniques, page 152); work wraps together with wrapped sts as you come to them.

*Short Row 1 (RS): K15 (17, 19), wrp-t.
Short Row 2: P14 (16, 18), wrp-t.
Short Row 3: K13 (15, 17), wrp-t.
Short Row 4: P12 (14, 16), wrp-t.
Short Row 5: K11 (13, 15), wrp-t.
Short Row 6: P10 (12, 14), wrp-t.
Short Row 7: K9 (11, 13), wrp-t.
Short Row 8: P8 (10, 12), wrp-t.

SIZES 6–12 AND 12–18 MONTHS ONLY

Short Row 9: K– (9, 11), wrp-t.
Short Row 10: P– (8, 10), wrp-t.

SIZE 12–18 MONTHS ONLY

Short Row 11: K9, wrp-t.
Short Row 12: P8, wrp-t.

ALL SIZES

Short Row 13: K9, wrp-t.
Short Row 14: P10, wrp-t.
Short Row 15: K11, wrp-t.
Short Row 16: P12, wrp-t.
Short Row 17: K13, wrp-t.
Short Row 18: P14, wrp-t.

SIZES 6–12 AND 12–18 MONTHS ONLY

Short Row 19: K15, wrp-t.
Short Row 20: P16, wrp-t.

SIZE 12–18 MONTHS ONLY

Short Row 21: K17, wrp-t.
Short Row 22: P18, wrp-t.**

ALL SIZES

Next Row (RS): Carefully unravel Provisional CO and place live sts on spare needle. Slip 1, knit to last st, k1-tbl, knit across sts from Provisional CO—32 (36, 40) sts.

Join for working in the rnd; pm for beginning of rnd. Knit 4 rnds.
Next Rnd: K3, BO next 12 sts, knit to end, remove beginning-of-rnd marker, k3—20 (24, 28) sts remain.

FOOT

Working back and forth, knit 1 row.
Increase Row 1 (RS): Slip 1, k1-f/b, knit to last 2 sts, k1-f/b, k1—22 (26, 30) sts. Purl 1 row.
Increase Row 2: Slip 1, k1-f/b, knit to last 2 sts, k1-f/b, k1—24 (28, 32) sts. Work even in St st for 3 rows.

HEEL

Note: Heel is shaped using short rows; work wraps together with wrapped sts as you come to them.
Short Row 1 (RS): K20 (23, 26), wrp-t.
Short Row 2: P16 (18, 20), wrp-t.
Repeat from * to ** as for Toe.

HEEL FLAP

Next Row (RS): Knit to end, pick up bar after wrapped st and knit together with next st to close gap. Purl 1 row, pick up bar after wrapped st and purl together with next st to close gap.
Decrease Row 1 (RS): Slip 1, k4 (5, 6), k2tog, k10 (12, 14), k2tog, k5 (6, 7)—22 (26, 30) sts remain. Purl 1 row.
Decrease Row 2: Slip 1, k4 (5, 6), k2tog, k9 (11, 13), k2tog, p4 (5, 6)—20 (24, 28) sts remain. Purl 1 row.
Decrease Row 3: Slip 1, k3 (4, 5), k2tog, k8 (10, 12), k2tog, k4 (5, 6)—18 (22, 26) sts remain. Purl 1 row. Knit 1 row. Purl 1 row. BO all sts.

STRAP

Pick up and knit 5 sts along side edge of Heel Flap.
Note: When picking up sts for Strap for second Bootie, make sure to pick them up on opposite side edge of Heel Flap so that you have a left and right Bootie.
Begin St st, beginning with a purl row; work even for 19 (21, 23) rows.
Buttonhole Row (RS): K4 sts, BO last st knit, k1.
Next Row: Purl, CO 1 st over BO st. Knit 1 row. Purl 1 row.
Next Row (RS): K2tog, k1, k2tog—3 sts remain. BO all sts purlwise.

FINISHING

Felting
Felt piece well by hand (see page 14) [1].

Sew button opposite buttonhole on Strap.

Embroidery
Using embroidery needle and 2 strands of embroidery floss held together, embroider flower using Lazy Daisy for the petals and 3 French knots for the center (see Guide below) [2].

Soling
Add soling of your choice (see page 18). I used a sewn-on suede sole for mine.

- - - - - - - - { FLOWER GUIDE } - - - - - - - -

- - - - { BEFORE AND AFTER FELTING } - - - -

[1] Notice how much size and fabric density change after felting.

- - - { EMBROIDERING FLOWER ON BOOTIE } - - -

[2] Using embroidery needle and 2 strands of embroidery floss held together, embroider flower (left).

Garter-stitch bands and tie cords give these simple, feminine slippers
structure and style. A quick-to-knit gift for your budding ballerina!

SIZES
Child's X-Small (Small, Medium, Large)

FINISHED MEASUREMENTS
6 (7, 8, 9)" [15 (18, 20.5, 23) cm] Foot length

YARN
Peace Fleece Worsted [75% wool / 25% mohair; 200 yards (183 meters) / 4 ounces (114 grams)]: 1 hank Mourning Dove

NEEDLES
One set of five double-pointed needles (dpn) size US 7 (4.5 mm); change needle size if necessary to obtain correct gauge

GAUGE
18 sts and 20 rows = 4" (10 cm) in Stockinette stitch (St st)

OVERVIEW
The Sole is worked back and forth, with increases for the toe and heel. Stitches are bound off for the foot opening, then the heel Tab is worked for a few rows. I-Cord Ties are worked, then threaded though the Tabs.

SLIPPER
CO 24 (32, 40, 40) sts. Knit 1 row.

Shape Slipper
Increase Row 1: K2, k1-f/b, k1 (2, 3, 3), k1-f/b, k2 (3, 4, 4), [k1-f/b, k1 (2, 3, 3)] twice, [k1-f/b] twice, [k1 (2, 3, 3), k1-f/b] twice, k2 (3, 4, 4), k1-f/b, k1 (2, 3, 3), k1-f/b, k2—34 (42, 50, 50) sts. Knit 1 (2, 2, 2) row(s).
Increase Row 2: K2, k1-f/b, k1 (2, 3, 3), k1-f/b, k7 (8, 9, 9), [k1-f/b, k1 (2, 3, 3)] twice, [k1-f/b] twice, [k1 (2, 3, 3), k1-f/b] twice, k7 (8, 9, 9), k1-f/b, k1 (2, 3, 3), k1-f/b, k2—44 (52, 60, 60) sts. Knit 2 rows.

SIZE LARGE ONLY
Increase Row 3: K2, k1-f/b, k5, k1-f/b, k10, k1-f/b, k5, k1-f/b, k3, [k1-f/b] twice, k3, k1-f/b, k5, k1-f/b, k10, k1-f/b, k5, k1-f/b, k2—70 sts. Knit 1 row.

ALL SIZES
Increase Row 4: K18 (22, 26, 31), k1-f/b, k2, [k1-f/b] twice, k2, k1-f/b, k18 (22, 26, 31)—48 (56, 64, 74) sts. Knit 1 row. Purl 1 row. Knit 4 (4, 6, 6) rows.
Decrease Row 1: K16 (20, 22, 27), [k2tog, k1 (1, 2, 2)] twice, [k2tog] twice, [k1 (1, 2, 2), k2tog] twice, k16 (20, 22, 27)—42 (50, 58, 68) sts remain.

Decrease Row 2: P2, p2tog, p9 (13, 15, 20), [p2tog, p1 (1, 2, 2)] twice, [p2tog] twice, [p1 (1, 2, 2), p2tog] twice, p9 (13, 15, 20), p2tog, p2—34 (42, 50, 60) sts remain. Knit 2 rows.
Decrease Row 3: K12 (16, 19, 24), k2tog, k1 (1, 2, 2), [k2tog] twice, k1 (1, 2, 2), k2tog, k12 (16, 19, 24)—30 (38, 46, 56) sts remain.
Bind-Off Row: K1, BO next 27 (35, 43, 53) sts, knit to end—3 sts remain, including 1 st at beginning of row. Fold piece in half widthwise; sew CO edges together, then sew side edges.

TAB
Work even in Garter st (knit every row) for 12 rows. BO all sts. Fold Tab over to WS and sew BO end to WS of top of Slipper.

FINISHING
I-Cord Ties (make 2)
Using dpns, CO 3 sts. Work I-Cord 30" (76 cm) long (see Special Techniques, page 152). Thread one Tie through each Tab.

Soling
Add soling (see page 18) of your choice. Sample shown with paint-on latex soling.

These two-toned clog-style slippers are snug like shoes, but cozier. You can make clogs for everyone in your family as this pattern is sized for children and adults. To create the two-toned effect, you knit and felt two identical pieces, then slip one inside the other. They work up quickly at such a loose gauge, and the double layering makes them trim yet cozy.

SIZES
Child's X-Small (Child's Small, Child's Medium, Child's Large/Women's Small, Women's Medium/Men's Small, Women's Large/Men's Medium, Men's Large)

FINISHED MEASUREMENTS
8 (9, 10, 11, 12, 13, 14)" [20.5 (23, 25.5, 28, 30.5, 33, 35.5) cm] circumference, before felting
6 (6½, 7, 7½, 8, 9, 10)" [15 (16.5, 18, 19, 20.5, 23, 25.5) cm] circumference, after felting
8¼ (8½, 10¼, 10¾, 11½, 13, 13½)" [21 (21.5, 26, 27.5, 29, 33, 34.5) cm] length, before felting, from beginning of Gusset to tip of Toe
6 (7, 8, 9, 10, 11, 12)" [15 (18, 20.5, 23, 25.5, 28, 30.5) cm] length, after felting

YARN
Cascade Yarns Cascade 220 Heathers [100% Peruvian Highland wool; 220 yards (201 meters) / 100 grams]: 1 (1, 1, 1, 1, 2, 2) hank(s) each MC and A
Men's Version: #9564 Birch Heather (MC) and #8012 Doeskin Heather (A); Women's Version: #2433 Pacific (MC) and #2447 Peacock (A)

NEEDLES
One set of five double-pointed needles (dpn) size US 10½ (6.5 mm); change needle size if necessary to obtain correct gauge

NOTIONS
Stitch marker; newsprint; paint-on latex or soling material of your choice

GAUGE
16 sts and 20 rnds = 4" (10 cm) in Stockinette stitch (St st), before felting

OVERVIEW

The Heel Flap and Gusset are worked back and forth, then stitches are cast on for the Instep, and the Instep and shaped Toe are worked in the round. Each Clog is made of 1 piece in each color; the pieces are felted, and one is inserted inside the other.

CLOG (Make 2 in MC and 2 in A)
HEEL FLAP

CO 8 (9, 10, 11, 12, 13, 14) sts. Do not join.
Row 1: (RS) Knit.
Row 2: Slip 1 purlwise, purl to end.
Row 3: Slip 1 knitwise, knit to end.
Repeat Rows 2 and 3 four (5, 6, 7, 8, 9, 10) times.

Turn Heel

Note: Heel is shaped using short rows (see Special Techniques, page 152); work wraps together with wrapped sts as you come to them.
Short Row 1 (WS): P7 (8, 9, 10, 11, 12, 13), wrp-t.
Short Row 2: K6 (7, 8, 9, 10, 11, 12), wrp-t.
Short Row 3: P5 (6, 7, 8, 9, 10, 11), wrp-t.
Short Row 4: K4 (5, 6, 7, 8, 9, 10), wrp-t.
Continue working short rows as established, working 1 less st on each row before wrp-t, until you have worked 1 (2, 3, 4, 5, 6, 7) additional row(s). On the final row, you should have worked 3 sts before working wrp-t.

SIZES CHILD'S SMALL, CHILD'S LARGE/WOMEN'S SMALL, AND WOMEN'S LARGE/MEN'S MEDIUM ONLY

Final Short Row: P3, wrp-t.

GUSSET
ALL SIZES

Set-Up Row 1 (RS): K5 (6, 6, 7, 7, 8, 8), pick up and knit 6 (7, 8, 9, 10, 11, 12) sts, picking up sts from slipped Heel Flap sts—14 (16, 18, 20, 22, 24, 26) sts.
Set-Up Row 2: Purl to end, pick up and knit 6 (7, 8, 9, 10, 11, 12) sts, picking up sts from Slipped Heel Flap sts—20 (23, 26, 29, 32, 35, 38) sts. Work even in St st for 1 (1, 1, 3, 3, 3, 3) row(s), slipping first st of every row.
Decrease Row (WS): Slip 1, p1, p2tog, purl to last 4 sts, p2tog, p2—18 (21, 24, 27, 30, 33, 36) sts remain.
Next Row: Slip 1, knit to end.
Repeat last 2 rows twice— 14 (17, 20, 23, 26, 29, 32) sts

remain. Work even for 2 (2, 2, 4, 4, 6, 6) rows.
Increase Row (WS): Slip 1, [p1-f/b] twice, purl to last 3 sts, [p1-f/b] twice, p1 — 18 (21, 24, 27, 30, 33, 36) sts.
Next Row: Slip 1, knit to end.
Repeat last 2 rows twice—26 (29, 32, 35, 38, 41, 44) sts.

INSTEP

Using Backward Loop CO (see Special Techniques, page 152), CO 6 (7, 8, 9, 10, 11, 12) sts—32 (36, 40, 44, 48, 52, 56) sts. Join for working in the rnd; pm for beginning of rnd. Knit 7 (8, 9, 10, 11, 12, 13) rnds.
*Decrease Rnd: Knit to last 8 sts, k2tog, knit to last 2 sts, k2tog—30 (34, 38, 42, 46, 50, 54) sts remain. Knit 1 (1, 1, 2, 2, 3, 3) rnd(s).
Repeat from * twice—26 (30, 34, 38, 42, 46, 50) sts remain. Knit 3 (4, 5, 4, 5, 5, 6) rnds.

TOE

Note: Toe is shaped using short row (see Special Techniques, page 152); work wraps together with wrapped sts as you come to them.

SIZE CHILD'S X-SMALL ONLY
Short Row 1 (RS): K1, wrp-t.
Short Row 2 (WS): P8, wrp-t.
Short Row 3: Knit to end.
Rnds 4, 9, and 11: Knit.
Short Rows 5–7: Repeat Short Rows 1–3.
Rnd 8 (Decrease Rnd): K2tog, knit to end—25 sts remain.
Rnd 10 (Decrease Rnd): *K3, k2tog; repeat from * to end—20 sts remain.
Rnd 12 (Decrease Rnd): *K2, k2tog; repeat from * to end— 15 sts remain.

SIZE CHILD'S SMALL ONLY
Short Row 1 (RS): K1, wrp-t.
Short Row 2 (WS): P9, wrp-t.
Short Row 3: Knit to end.
Rnds 4, 9, and 11: Knit.

Short Rows 5-7: Repeat Short Rows 1-3.
Rnd 8 (Decrease Rnd): *K4, k2tog; repeat from * to end—25 sts remain.
Rnd 10 (Decrease Rnd): *K3, k2tog; repeat from * to end—20 sts remain.
Rnd 12 (Decrease Rnd): *K2, k2tog; repeat from * to end—15 sts remain.

SIZE CHILD'S MEDIUM ONLY
Short Row 1 (RS): K1, wrp-t.
Short Row 2 (WS): P10, wrp-t.
Short Row 3: Knit to end.
Rnds 4, 9, 14, and 16: Knit.
Short Rows 5-7: Repeat Short Rows 1-3.
Rnd 8 (Decrease Rnd): *K5, k2tog; repeat from * to last 6 sts, knit to end—30 sts remain.
Short Row 10 (RS): K1, wrp-t.
Short Row 11 (WS): P10, wrp-t.
Short Row 12: Knit to end.
Rnd 13 (Decrease Rnd): *K4, k2tog; repeat from * to end—25 sts remain.
Rnd 15 (Decrease Rnd): *K3, k2tog; repeat from * to end—20 sts remain.
Rnd 17 (Decrease Rnd): *K2, k2tog; repeat from * to end—15 sts remain.

SIZE CHILD'S LARGE/WOMEN'S SMALL ONLY
Short Row 1 (RS): K1, wrp-t.
Short Row 2 (WS): P11, wrp-t.
Short Row 3: Knit to end.
Rnds 4, 9, 11, 16, and 18: Knit.
Short Rows 5-7: Repeat Short Rows 1-3.
Rnd 8 (Decrease Rnd): *K8, k2tog; repeat from * to last 8 sts, knit to end—35 sts remain.
Rnd 10 (Decrease Rnd): *K5, k2tog; repeat from * to end—30 sts remain.
Short Row 12 (RS): K1, wrp-t.
Short Row 13 (WS): P11, wrp-t.
Short Row 14: Knit to end.
Rnd 15 (Decrease Rnd): *K4, k2tog; repeat from * to

end—25 sts remain.
Rnd 17 (Decrease Rnd): *K3, k2tog; repeat from * to end—20 sts remain.
Rnd 19 (Decrease Rnd): *K2, k2tog; repeat from * to end—15 sts remain.

SIZE WOMEN'S MEDIUM/MEN'S SMALL ONLY
Rnd 1 (Decrease Rnd): K4, k2tog, k20, k2tog, knit to end—40 sts remain.
Rnds 2, 7, 12, 17, and 19: Knit.
Short Row 3 (RS): K1, wrp-t.
Short Row 4 (WS): P12, wrp-t.
Short Row 5: Knit to end.
Rnd 6 (Decrease Rnd): *K6, k2tog; repeat from * to end—35 sts remain.
Short Rows 8-10: Repeat Short Rows 3-5.
Rnd 11 (Decrease Rnd): *K5, k2tog; repeat from * to end—30 sts remain.
Short Row 13 (RS): K1, wrp-t.
Short Row 14 (WS): P12, wrp-t.
Short Row 15: Knit to end.
Rnd 16 (Decrease Rnd): *K4, k2tog; repeat from * to end—25 sts remain.
Rnd 18 (Decrease Rnd): *K3, k2tog; repeat from * to end—20 sts remain.
Rnd 20 (Decrease Rnd): *K2, k2tog; repeat from * to end—15 sts remain.

SIZE WOMEN'S LARGE/MEN'S MEDIUM ONLY
Rnd 1 (Decrease Rnd): K2tog, knit to end—45 sts remain.
Rnds 2, 7, 12, 17, 22, and 24: Knit.
Short Row 3 (RS): K1, wrp-t.
Short Row 4 (WS): P13, wrp-t.
Short Row 5: Knit to end.
Rnd 6 (Decrease Rnd): *K7, k2tog; repeat from * to end—40 sts remain.
Short Rows 8-10: Repeat Short Rows 3-5.
Rnd 11 (Decrease Rnd): *K6, k2tog; repeat from * to end—35 sts remain.

Short Rows 13-15: Repeat Short Rows 3-5.
Rnd 16 (Decrease Rnd): *K5, k2tog; repeat from * to end—30 sts remain.
Short Row 18 (RS): K1, wrp-t.
Short Row 19 (WS): P13, wrp-t.
Short Row 20: Knit to end.
Rnd 21 (Decrease Rnd): *K4, k2tog; repeat from * to end—25 sts remain.
Rnd 23 (Decrease Rnd): *K3, k2tog; repeat from * to end—20 sts remain.
Rnd 25 (Decrease Rnd): *K2, k2tog; repeat from * to end—15 sts remain.

SIZE MEN'S LARGE ONLY
Rnds 1, 3, 8, 13, 18, 23, and 25: Knit.
Rnd 2 (Decrease Rnd): *K8, k2tog; repeat from * to end—45 sts remain.
Short Row 4 (RS): K1, wrp-t.
Short Row 5 (WS): P14, wrp-t.
Short Row 6: Knit to end.
Rnd 7 (Decrease Rnd): *K7, k2tog; repeat from * to end—40 sts remain.
Short Rows 9-11: Repeat Short Rows 4-6.
Rnd 12 (Decrease Rnd): *K6, k2tog; repeat from * to end—35 sts remain.
Short Rows 14-16: Repeat Short Rows 4-6.
Rnd 17 (Decrease Rnd): *K5, k2tog; repeat from * to end—30 sts remain.
Short Row 19 (RS): K1, wrp-t.
Short Row 20 (WS): P14, wrp-t.
Short Row 21: Knit to end.
Rnd 22 (Decrease Rnd): *K4, k2tog; repeat from * to end—25 sts remain.
Rnd 24 (Decrease Rnd): *K3, k2tog; repeat from * to end—20 sts remain.
Rnd 26 (Decrease Rnd): *K2, k2tog; repeat from * to end—15 sts remain.

ALL SIZES
Cut yarn, leaving an 8" (20.5 cm) tail. Thread tail through remaining sts, pull tight, and fasten off [1].

----- { BEFORE AND AFTER FELTING } -----

[1] Completed Clogs, before felting.

[2] Completed wet Clogs, after felting.

FINISHING

Felt Clog to measurements (see page 14) [2]. While pieces are still damp, insert Color A Clog into MC Clog. Stuff Toe with newsprint [3], rounding it to a pleasing shape and pushing newsprint into Toe to create the traditional Clog profile [4]. Stuff Instep and Heel, tugging piece to finished length [5]. Allow to dry thoroughly.

Soling

Paint soles with liquid latex (see page 18).

- - - - { SHAPING CLOGS / COLOR A CLOG } - - - -

[3] While still damp, insert Color A Clog into MC Clog and stuff with newsprint.

[4] Round the toe into a pleasing shape and push newsprint into Toe to create traditional Clog profile.

[5] Stuff Instep and Heel, tugging piece to finished length.

A double-thick body and a generous (to say the least) wool cuff make these slippers extra warm and cozy. The statement cuff is made with yarn from an unraveled thrift-store sweater. These dramatically fringed slippers are super popular with both children and adults.

SIZES
Child's X-Small (Child's Small, Child's Medium, Child's Large/Women's Small, Women's Medium/Men's Small, Women's Large/Men's Medium, Men's Large)

FINISHED MEASUREMENTS
7 (8, 9, 9¾, 10¾, 11½, 12½)" [18 (20.5, 23, 25, 27, 29, 32) cm] Foot circumference, before finishing; circumference will shrink slightly after assembly
6 (7, 8, 9, 10, 11, 12)" [15 (18, 20.5, 23, 25.5, 28, 30.5) cm] Foot length

YARN
Malabrigo Merino Worsted [100% wool; 210 yards (192 meters) / 100 grams)]: 2 hanks #35 Frank Ochre

NEEDLES
One set of five double-pointed needles (dpn) size US 7 (4.5 mm); change needle size if necessary to obtain correct gauge

NOTIONS
Crochet hook size US H/8 (5mm) or one size larger; waste yarn; stitch marker; sweater to recycle with an approximate gauge of 18 sts and 28 rows = 4" (10 cm); sewing needle and thread

GAUGE
18 sts and 28 rows = 4" (10 cm) in Stockinette stitch (St st)

OVERVIEW

Two complete pieces are worked for each Slipper, then joined together at the top of the Cuff. The short knitted Cuff is worked in the round, then the Heel Flap is shaped using short rows. The Foot and shaped Toe are worked in the round. The Fringed Cuff is created from an unraveled thrift-store sweater.

SLIPPER (Make 4)
CUFF

Using Provisional CO (see Special Techniques, page 152), CO 32 (36, 40, 44, 48, 52, 56) sts. Divide sts among 4 dpns. Join for working in the rnd, being careful not to twist sts; pm for beginning of rnd. Begin St st (knit every rnd); work even for 7 (7, 9, 9, 9, 11, 11) rnds.

HEEL FLAP

Note: Heel Flap is shaped using short rows (see Special Techniques, page 152); work wraps together with wrapped sts as you come to them.

Short Row 1 (RS): K 14 (16, 18, 20, 22, 24, 26), wrp-t.
Short Row 2 (WS): P 13 (15, 17, 19, 21, 23, 25), wrp-t.
Short Rows 3–10: Continuing in St st, work 1 less st on each row before working wrp-t, until there are 5 (7, 9, 11, 13, 15, 17) sts remaining between wraps, and there are 5 wraps on each side.
Short Row 11: K6 (8, 10, 12, 14, 16, 18) wrp-t.
Short Row 12: P7 (9, 11, 13, 15, 17, 19) wrp-t.
Short Rows 13–18: Continue working 1 more st on each row before working wrp-t, until you have 13 (15, 17, 19, 21, 23, 25) sts between wraps.
Short Row 19: Knit to end.

FOOT

Rejoin for working in the rnd; continuing in St st, work even until piece measures 5 (6, 7, 7¾, 8¾, 9½, 10½)" [12.5 (15, 18, 19.5, 22, 24, 26.5) cm], or ¾ (1, 1, 1¼, 1¼, 1½, 1½)" [2 (2.5, 2.5, 3, 3, 4, 4) cm] less than desired length from back of Heel.

Shape Toe
SIZES CHILD'S SMALL, CHILD'S LARGE/WOMEN'S SMALL, AND WOMEN'S LARGE/MEN'S MEDIUM ONLY
Decrease Rnd 1: *K- (7, -, 9, -,11, -), k2tog; repeat from * to end— - (32, -, 40, - 48, -) sts remain. Knit 1 rnd.

ALL SIZES
Decrease Rnd 2: *K2 (2, 3, 3, 4, 4, 5), k2tog; repeat from * to end—24 (24, 32, 32, 40, 40, 48) sts remain. Knit 1 rnd.
Decrease Rnd 3: K0 (0, 1, 1, 2, 2, 3), k2tog, *k1 (1, 2, 2, 3, 3, 4), k2tog; repeat from * to last st, k1 — 16 (16, 24, 24, 32, 32, 40) sts remain. Knit 1 rnd.
Decrease Rnd 4: *K0 (0, 1, 1, 2, 2, 3), k2tog; repeat from * to end—8 (8, 16, 16, 24, 24, 32) sts remain. Knit 0 (0, 1, 1, 1, 1, 1) rnd(s).

SIZES CHILD'S MEDIUM AND CHILD'S LARGE/WOMEN'S SMALL ONLY
Decrease Rnd 5: *K2tog; repeat from * to end—8 sts remain.

SIZES WOMEN'S MEDIUM/MEN'S SMALL, WOMEN'S LARGE/MEN'S MEDIUM, AND MEN'S LARGE ONLY
Decrease Rnd 6: K- (-, -, -, 0, 0, 1), k2tog, *k- (-, -, -, 1, 1, 2), k2tog: repeat from * to last st, k1 — - (-, -, -, 16, 16, 24) sts remain. Knit 1 rnd.
Decrease Rnd 7: *K- (-, -, -, 0, 0, 1), k2tog; repeat from * to end— - (-, -, -, 8, 8, 16) sts remain.

SIZE MEN'S LARGE ONLY
Knit 1 rnd.
Decrease Rnd 8: *K2tog; repeat from * to end— 8 sts remain.

ALL SIZES
Cut yarn, leaving a 6" (15 cm) tail; thread through remaining sts, pull tight, and fasten off.

FINISHING

Turn one Slipper inside out and slip it inside the other one. Line up beginning of rnd for each Slipper. Carefully unpick Provisional CO and transfer sts back to needles; using 3-Needle BO (see Special Techniques, page 152), join Cuffs.

Note: To make it easer to work the BO, you may want to unpick and transfer only a portion of the sts for each Slipper at one time.

Fringed Cuff

Cut 4 lengthwise pieces (i.e., cutting from top to bottom, not side to side) from sweater, 4" (10 cm) wide x 1" (2.5 cm) longer than Cuff measurement.

Note: If you'd like a less full Fringe Cuff, cut 3 pieces instead of 4.

Stack pieces together and, using a sewing machine, sew line down center, lengthwise. Sew second line on top of the first for reinforcement [1]. Unravel the knitting by pulling apart each row along edges on both sides to release sts and create fringe [2]. After you have pulled apart a few rows, you can begin pulling on the yarn to expedite the process [3]. Trim fringe, if desired, to make it shorter and more even. Using sewing needle and thread, sew sewn edge of Fringed Cuff to BO edge of Slipper Cuff.

Note: Spot clean body of Slipper only; do not wet Fringe or it will lose its curl.

[1] Cut 4 lengthwise pieces from sweater from top to bottom. Stack the 4 pieces, then machine-sew 2 lines, one on top of the other, lengthwise down center.

[2] To start making fringe, pull apart each row.

[3] Begin pulling on yarn to make fringe faster.

Chunky wool and garter stitch add to the rustic style of these children's boot slippers. Leather lacing ensures they stay on busy feet.

SIZES
Child's X-Small (Small, Medium, Large)

FINISHED MEASUREMENTS
7 1/4 (8, 8 1/2, 8 1/2)" [18.5 (20.5, 21.5, 21.5) cm] outside Slipper circumference
5 (5 1/4, 5 3/4, 5 3/4)" [12.5 (13.5, 14.5, 14.5) cm] Foot circumference
5 3/4 (7, 7 3/4, 9)" [14.5, (18, 19.5, 23) cm] Foot length

YARN
Brooklyn Tweed Shelter [100% Targhee-Columbia wool; 140 yards (128 meters) / 50 grams]: 1 hank #18 Button Jar

NEEDLES
One set of five double-pointed needles (dpn) size US 10 1/2 (6.5 mm); change needle size if necessary to obtain correct gauge

NOTIONS
Piece of suede large enough for 2 soles; double-sided tape; leather needle; embroidery floss or heavy-duty thread to match yarn; 2 yards (2 meters) length 1/8" (32 cm) wide leather lace

GAUGE
12 sts and 24 rows = 4" (10 cm) in Garter stitch (knit every row), using 2 strands of yarn held together

OVERVIEW
The Leg is worked back and forth to the Heel, with eyelets for the laces. The Heel is shaped using short rows. Additional stitches are cast on for the Foot, which is then worked back and forth to the shaped Toe. The Tongue is worked back and forth, then its bound-off edge is sewn to the stitches cast on for the Foot, and the side edges of the Foot are sewn together.

LEG
Using 2 strands of yarn held together, CO 18 (20, 22, 22) sts. Knit 3 rows.
Eyelet Row (RS): K2, yo, k2tog, knit to last 4 sts, k2tog, yo, k2. Knit 6 rows.
Repeat Eyelet Row every 7 rows 2 (2, 2, 3) times. Knit 4 rows.

HEEL

Note: Heel is shaped using short rows (see Special Techniques, page 152); since the piece is worked in Garter st, there is no need to work wraps together with wrapped sts.

Short Row 1 (RS): K14 (16, 18, 18), wrp-t.
Short Row 2: K10 (12, 14, 14), wrp-t.
Short Row 3: K9 (11, 13, 13), wrp-t.
Short Row 4: K8 (10, 12, 12), wrp-t.
Short Row 5: K7 (9, 11, 11), wrp-t.
Short Row 6: K6 (8, 10, 10), wrp-t.
Short Row 7: K5 (7, 9, 9), wrp-t.
Short Row 8: K4 (6, 8, 8), wrp-t.
Short Row 9: K5 (7, 9, 9), wrp-t.
Short Row 10: K6 (8, 10, 10), wrp-t.
Short Row 11: K7 (9, 11, 11), wrp-t.
Short Row 12: K8 (10, 12, 12), wrp-t.
Short Row 13: K9 (11, 13, 13), wrp-t.
Short Row 14: K10 (12, 14, 14) wrp-t.
Short Row 15: Knit across all sts. Pick up bar after wrapped sts and knit together with next st to close gap. Knit 1 row.
Next Row (RS): Using Backward Loop CO (see Special Techniques, page 151), CO 4 sts, knit across these sts, k2, yo, k2tog, knit to last 4 sts, k2tog, yo, k2—22 (24, 26, 26) sts. Cut yarn.

FOOT

Place last 9 (10, 11, 11) sts worked on empty needle. Rejoin yarn and knit across these sts, knit across 4 CO sts, knit to end. Knit 25 (32, 37, 44) rows.

TOE

SIZE X-SMALL ONLY
Decrease Row: [K9, k2tog] twice—20 sts remain. Knit 1 row.

SIZES MEDIUM AND LARGE ONLY
Decrease Row: [K11, k2tog] twice—24 sts remain. Knit 1 row.

SIZES SMALL, MEDIUM, AND LARGE ONLY
Decrease Row: [K3, k2tog, k2, k2tog, k3] twice—20 sts remain. Knit 1 row.

ALL SIZES
Decrease Row 1: [K2, k2tog, k2, k2tog, k2] twice—16 sts remain. Knit 1 row.
Decrease Row 2: [K1, k2tog, k2, k2tog, k1] twice—12 sts remain. Knit 1 row.
Decrease Row 3: *K2tog; repeat from * to end—6 sts remain. Cut yarn, leaving an 8" (20.5 cm) tail. Thread tail through remaining sts, pull tight, and fasten off.

TONGUE

Using 2 strands of yarn held together, CO 10 sts. Knit 23 (23, 23, 29) rows.
Bind-Off Row: Bind off 2 sts, knit to end, bind off last st—7 sts remain.

FINISHING

Sew BO edge of Tongue to CO sts at end of Heel shaping. Sew side edges of Foot together. Beginning at bottom eyelets, thread leather cord through eyelets as for a shoe.

Soling

Add soling of your choice (see page 18). I used a sewn-on suede sole for mine.

Every year at our local fiber festival, I admire the rich colorways of the hand-dyed wool roving on offer, and I couldn't resist incorporating some into these booties. I knit the booties flat using a sturdy yarn, working the thrums as I went. I love the way the bright roving contrasts with the rustic gray yarn on the outside; while inside, the roving forms a soft, squishy, very warm lining. Over time the thrums will felt together on the inner sole, creating an even footbed.

SIZES
Child's X-Small (Child's Small, Child's Medium, Child's Large/Women's Small, Women's Medium/Men's Small, Women's Large/Men's Medium, Men's Large)

FINISHED MEASUREMENTS
6 (7 1/4, 8 1/4, 10, 11 1/4, 12 1/4, 12 1/4)" [15 (18.5, 21, 25.5, 28.5, 31, 31) cm] circumference at ball of foot
7 (8, 9 1/4, 9 3/4, 10 3/4, 11, 12)" [18 (20.5, 23.5, 25, 27, 28, 30.5) cm] Foot length, from back of Slipper

YARN
Rowan PureLife British Sheep Breeds Chunky Undyed (100% British wool; 120 yards (110 meters) / 100 grams): 1 (1, 1, 2, 2, 2) skein(s) #952 Mid Brown Jacob

Madame Zabet's Floofalicious Fiber Bluefaced Leicester Wool Roving (100% wool); 3 ounces [85 grams] Carmen Miranda

NEEDLES
One pair straight needles size US 8 (5 mm); change needle size if necessary to obtain correct gauge.

NOTIONS
Stitch marker; leather needle; embroidery floss to match yarn; double-sided tape

GAUGE
14 sts and 18 rows = 4" (10 cm) in Stockinette stitch (St st)

OVERVIEW
These Booties are worked back and forth with minimal shaping at the toe, then the side edges are sewn together from the toe to the desired location of the cuff opening.

ABBREVIATIONS
T1: Thrum 1 st as follows: The thrums are created by taking short pieces of roving and knitting them in as you work. They appear as big puffy stitches on the outside and fleecy ends on the inside. To prepare roving for making thrums, divide the roving into strips 2 to 3 times the width of MC yarn, then pull off 4" (10 cm) lengths to knit as thrums. When you want to place a thrum, fold both ends to the middle and twist it a bit at the middle section. Insert the right-hand needle into the next stitch, loop the folded thrum over the needle as you would to wrap a stitch when knitting, and draw the thrum through the stitch and off the left-hand needle. Run the working yarn behind the stitch, ready to knit the following stitch.

BOOTIES

CO 29 (33, 41, 45, 49, 53, 57) sts.

Row (RS) 1: Knit.

Row 2 and All WS Rows: Purl.

Row 3: K4, T1, *k3, T1; repeat from * to last 4 sts, k4.

Row 5: K1, ssk, knit to last 3 sts, k2tog, k1—27 (31, 39, 43, 47, 51, 55) sts remain.

Row 7: K5, T1, *k3, T1; repeat from * to last 5 sts, k5.

Row 9: Knit.

Row 11: K1, ssk, T1, *k3, T1; repeat from * to last 3 sts, k2tog, k1—25 (29, 37, 41, 45, 49, 53) sts remain.

Row 13: Knit.

Row 15: K4, T1, *k3, T1; repeat from * to last 4 sts, k4.

Row 17: K1, ssk, knit to last 3 sts, k2tog, k1—23 (27, 35, 39, 43, 47, 51) sts remain.

Row 19: K1, T1, *k3, T1; repeat from * to last st, k1.

Row 21: Knit.

Row 23: K1, ssk, T1, *k3, T1; repeat from * to last 3 sts, k2tog, k1—21 (25, 33, 37, 41, 45, 49) sts remain.

Row 25: Knit.

Row 27: K4, T1, *k3, T1; repeat from * to last 4 sts, k4.

Row 29: K1, ssk, knit to last 3 sts, k2tog, k1—19 (23, 31, 35, 39, 43, 47) sts remain.

Row 30: Purl.

SIZES CHILD'S SMALL, CHILD'S MEDIUM, CHILD'S LARGE/WOMEN'S SMALL, WOMEN'S MEDIUM/MEN'S SMALL, WOMEN'S LARGE/MEN'S MEDIUM, AND MEN'S LARGE ONLY

Row 31: K1, T1, *k3, T1; repeat from * to last st, k1.

Row 33: Knit.

Row 34: Purl.

SIZES CHILD'S MEDIUM, CHILD'S LARGE/WOMEN'S SMALL, WOMEN'S MEDIUM/MEN'S SMALL, WOMEN'S LARGE/MEN'S MEDIUM, AND MEN'S LARGE ONLY

Row 35: K1, ssk, T1, *k3, T1; repeat from * to last 3 sts, k2tog, k1— – (–, 29, 33, 37, 41, 45) sts remain.

Row 37: Knit.

Row 39: K1, ssk, knit to last 3 sts, k2tog, k1— – (–, 27, 31, 35, 39, 43) sts remain.

Row 40: Purl.

SIZES CHILD'S LARGE/WOMEN'S SMALL, WOMEN'S MEDIUM/MEN'S SMALL, WOMEN'S LARGE/MEN'S MEDIUM, AND MEN'S LARGE ONLY

Row 41: K1, T1, *k3, T1; repeat from * to last st, k1.

Row 42: Purl.

SIZES WOMEN'S MEDIUM/MEN'S SMALL, WOMEN'S LARGE/MEN'S MEDIUM, AND MEN'S LARGE ONLY

Row 43: Knit.

Row 45: K1, ssk, K1, T1, *k3, T1; repeat from * to last 3 sts, k2tog, k1— – (–, –, –, 33, 37, 41) sts.

Row 46: Purl.

SIZES WOMEN'S LARGE/MEN'S MEDIUM AND MEN'S LARGE ONLY

Row 47: Knit.

Row 48: Purl.

SIZE MEN'S LARGE ONLY

Row 49: K4, T1, *k3, T1; repeat from * to last 4 sts, k4.

Row 51: K1, ssk, knit to last 3 sts, k2tog, k1—39 sts remain.

ALL SIZES

Next Row (RS): K2 (0, 0, 2, 0, 2, 0), *k1, k2tog; repeat from * to last 2 (2, 0, 2, 0, 2, 0) sts, knit to end—14 (16, 18, 22, 22, 26, 26) sts remain.

Final Row: *P2tog; repeat from * to end—7 (8, 9, 11, 11, 13, 13) sts remain. Cut yarn, leaving an 8" (20.5 cm) tail. Thread tail through remaining sts, pull tight, and fasten off.

{ SEWING TOP AND BACK SEAMS }

[1] Sew side edges together for approximately ½ to ⅔ of length.

[2] For back seam, with WSs of CO edges together, work Running st up back edge, ¼" (6.5 cm) in from back edge.

FINISHING

For top seam, beginning at Final Row, sew side edges together for approximately one half to two thirds of the length, leaving the remaining length open for your ankle [1]. *Note: You may wish to try on the Bootie first, then mark the desired end of the seam, making sure to allow enough room to comfortably slide foot into Bootie.* For back seam, with WSs of CO edges together, work running st (see Special Techniques, page 152) up back edge, ¼" (.5 cm) in from back edge [2].

Soling

Add partial suede sole for bottom of Booties, following Templates at right (see page 152), or use soling method of your choice.

{ TEMPLATES FOR PARTIAL SUEDE SOLE FOR BOTTOM OF BOOTIE }

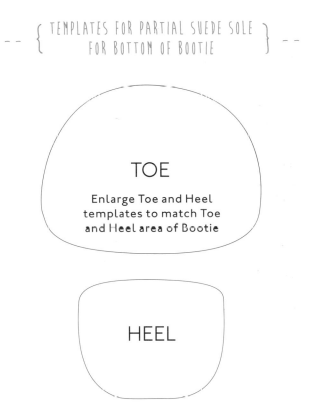

TOE

Enlarge Toe and Heel templates to match Toe and Heel area of Bootie

HEEL

These scuffs are just the thing for puttering around the house on a Sunday morning or any lazy day. They have a double helping of wool: The sturdy outer layer is worked with two strands of worsted-weight yarn; the plush, loopy lining is worked from chunky single-ply yarn.

SIZES
Women's Small (Women's Medium/Men's Small, Women's Large/Men's Medium, Men's Large)

FINISHED MEASUREMENTS
10¾ (12, 13¼, 14)" [27.5, (30.5, 33.5, 35.5) cm] Foot circumference, before felting
8 (9, 10, 10½)" [20.5 (23, 25.5, 26.5) cm] Foot inside circumference, after felting
15¾ (17¾, 19¾, 20½)" [40 (45, 50, 54.5) cm] Foot length, before felting
9 (10, 11, 12)" [23 (25.5, 28, 30.5) cm] Foot length, after felting

YARN
Casade Yarns Cascade 220 Heathers (100% Peruvian highland wool; 220 yards [201 meters] / 100 grams): 2 (2, 2, 3) hanks #9442 Baby Rose Heather (MC)
Brown Sheep Burly Spun [100% wool; 132 yards (120 meters) / 8 ounces (228 grams)]: 1 hank #BS10 Cream (A)

NEEDLES
One set of five double-pointed needles (dpn) size US 13 (9 mm); one pair straight needles size US 11 (8 mm); change needle size if necessary to obtain correct gauge

NOTIONS
Stitch marker; newsprint; disposable razor; large-eye sewing needle and embroidery floss or heavy-duty thread to match MC and A; double-thick chipboard; utility knife; paint-on latex or soling material of your choice

GAUGE
12 sts and 14 rows = 4" (10 cm) in Stockinette stitch (St st), using larger needles and 2 strands of MC held together, before felting
12 sts and 12 rows = 4" (10 cm) in pattern for Footbed, using smaller needles and A

OVERVIEW
The Sole is worked back and forth, then stitches are cast on for the Upper, and the Upper and shaped Toe are worked in the round. The Footbed and Trim are worked back and forth separately, then sewn to the Scuff.

ABBREVIATIONS
LS (Loop Stitch): K1, leaving st on left-hand needle; bring yarn between needles to the front, wrap around thumb once, then bring to the back; knit st on left-hand needle again, slipping it from left-hand needle; pass second st over first and off the needle, locking loop in place.

BODY

SOLE

Using larger needles and 2 strands of MC held together, CO 8 (8, 10, 10) sts. Begin St st; work even for 2 rows.

Shape Sole

Increase Row (RS): Increase 1 st each side this row, then every other row once, as follows: K 1, k 1-f/b, knit to last 2 sts, k 1-f/b, k 1—12 (12, 14, 14) sts. Work even for 9 (12, 14, 17) rows.

UPPER

Using Backward Loop CO (see Special Techniques, page 151), CO 16 (20, 21, 22) sts at beginning of row—28 (32, 35, 36) sts. Join for working in the rnd, being careful not to twist sts; pm for beginning of rnd. Knit 3 rnds.
Next Rnd: *K6 (7, 6, 5), k 1-f/b; repeat from * to end—32 (36, 40, 42) sts. Knit 28 (32, 35, 38) rnds.

Shape Upper
SIZES WOMEN'S SMALL, WOMEN'S LARGE/MEN'S MEDIUM, AND MEN'S LARGE ONLY

Decrease Rnd: *K14 (–, 8, 5), k2tog; repeat from * to end—30 (–, 36, 36) sts remain. Knit 1 rnd.

Shape Toe
SIZES WOMEN'S MEDIUM/MEN'S SMALL, WOMEN'S LARGE/MEN'S MEDIUM, AND MEN'S LARGE ONLY

Decrease Rnd: *K4, k2tog; repeat from * to end—30 sts remain. Knit 1 rnd.

ALL SIZES

Decrease Rnd 1: *K3, k2tog; repeat from * to end—24 sts remain. Knit 1 rnd.
Decrease Rnd 2: *K2, k2tog; repeat from * to end—18 sts remain. Knit 1 rnd.
Decrease Rnd 3: *K1, k2tog; repeat from * to end—12 sts remain. Knit 1 rnd.
Decrease Rnd 4: *K2tog; repeat from * to end—6 sts remain. Cut yarn, leaving an 8" (20.5 cm) tail. Thread tail through remaining sts, pull tight, and fasten off.

FOOTBED

Using smaller needles and A, CO 5 (5, 7, 7) sts.
Row 1 (RS): *LS; repeat from * to end.

Row 2: K 1, k 1-f/b, knit to last 3 sts, k 1-f/b, k 1—7 (7, 9, 9) sts.
Rows 3 and 4: Repeat Rows 1 and 2—9 (9, 11, 11) sts.
Row 5: Repeat Row 1.
Row 6: Knit.
Repeat Rows 5 and 6 until piece measures 7 1/2 (8 1/2, 9 1/2, 10 1/2)" [19 (21.5, 24, 26.5) cm], or to 1 1/2" (4 cm) less than desired length, ending with a RS row.
Decrease Row (WS): K 1, k2tog, knit to last 3 sts, k2tog, k 1—7 (7, 9, 9) sts remain.
Next Row: *LS; repeat from * to end.
Repeat Decrease Row once—5 (5, 7, 7) sts remain.
BO all sts, working LS as you BO.

TRIM (Make 2)

Using smaller needles and A, CO 16 (18, 20, 22) sts.
Row 1 (RS): *LS; repeat from * to end.
Row 2: Purl.
Repeat Rows 1 and 2 once.
BO all sts, working LS as you BO.

FINISHING

Felt Sole and Upper to measurements (see page 14).
Note: After felting, slipper must match lining size [1 and 2].
While piece is still damp, stuff with newsprint to form Upper. Round toe into pleasing shape and tug Sole to finished length. To remove excess fuzz, shave pieces with a disposable razor (see page 17). Allow to dry thoroughly.

Trace around Sole to determine size of chipboard insole. Draw cutting line 1/4" (.5 cm) in from traced edge [3]. Cut out along cutting lines; repeat for second slipper. Turn Body inside out and pin lining to Body with WSs of Body and Lining together. Using sewing needle and embroidery floss to match Body, sew lining to Upper, being careful not to let sts show on RS, and leaving heel end open to insert chipboard insole [4]. Turn Scuff RS out and insert chipboard insole. Sew heel closed. Using embroidery floss to match Trim, sew Trim to Upper [5].

Soling

Paint soles with liquid latex (see page 18).

----- { BEFORE AND AFTER FELTING } -----   ----- { MAKING LINING AND INSOLE } -----

[1] Unfelted Body before being felted to match size of lining.

[3] Trace around Sole to determine size of chipboard insole.

[2] Felted slipper now matches lining.

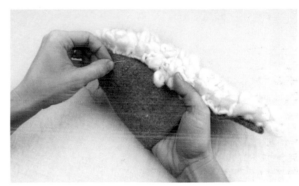

[4] Using emroidery floss, sew lining to inside of Body.

[5] Using embroidery floss, sew Trim to outside of Upper.

A thick felted sole stands in for the premade suede sole used for traditional slipper socks with this all-ages pattern. Knitted eyelets around the sole make it easy to pick up stitches for the quick-knit upper.

SIZES
Child's X-Small (Child's Small, Child's Medium, Child's Large/Women's Small, Women's Medium/Men's Small, Women's Large/Men's Medium, Men's Large)

FINISHED MEASUREMENTS
6 (7, 8, 9, 10, 11, 12)" [15 (18, 20.5, 23, 25.5, 28, 30.5) cm] Foot length

YARN
Cascade Yarns Cascade Magnum [100% Peruvian Highland wool; 123 yards (112 meters) / 250 grams): 1 (1, 1, 1, 1, 2, 2) hank(s) #9404 Ruby (MC)
Brown Sheep Lamb's Pride Worsted [85% wool / 15% mohair; 190 yards (174 meters) / 4 ounces (114 grams)]: 1 (1, 1, 1, 1, 2, 2) skein(s) #M07 Sable (A)

NEEDLES
One set of five double-pointed needles (dpn) size US 13 (9 mm); change needle size if necessary to obtain correct gauge.

NOTIONS
Crochet hook size US J/10 (6 mm); stitch marker; non-felting waste yarn; piece of shearling large enough to accommodate two linings; craft glue

GAUGE
10 sts and 12 rows = 4" (10 cm) in Stockinette stitch (St st), using 1 strand of MC
10 sts and 12 rows = 4" (10 cm) in St st, using 2 strands of A held together

STITCH PATTERN
2x2 Rib
(multiple of 4 sts; 1-rnd repeat)
All Rnds: *K2, p2; repeat from * to end.

OVERVIEW
The Sole is worked back and forth, with increases for toe and heel, then stitches on needle are joined and sides are worked in round. The cast-on edge is folded in half, and cast-on and side edges are sewn together. The Sole and sides are felted, then stitches for Upper are picked up from sides and worked in round, shaping along side edges of Foot. The Leg is worked from remaining stitches.

SOLE
Using 2 strands of A held together, CO 25 (32, 33, 40, 47, 48, 55) sts. Knit 1 row.

Shape Sole
Increase Row 1: K1, M1, k10 (14, 14, 18, 21, 22, 25), [M1, k1] twice, M1, k11 (14, 15, 18, 22, 22, 26), M1, k1—30 (37, 38, 45, 52, 53, 60) sts. Knit 1 row.

Increase Row 2: K1, M1, k13 (17, 17, 21, 24, 25, 28), [M1, k1] twice, M1, k13 (16, 17, 20, 24, 24, 28), M1, k1—35 (42, 43, 50, 57, 58, 65) sts. Knit 1 row.

Increase Row 3: K1, M1, k15 (19, 20, 23, 26, 27, 30), [M1, k1] twice, M1, k16 (19, 19, 23, 27, 27, 31), M1, k1—40 (47, 48, 55, 62, 63, 70) sts. Knit 1 row.

SIZES CHILD'S MEDIUM, CHILD'S LARGE/WOMEN'S SMALL, WOMEN'S MEDIUM/MEN'S SMALL, WOMEN'S LARGE/MEN'S MEDIUM, AND MEN'S LARGE ONLY
Increase Row 4: K1, M1, k- (-, 22, 26, 29, 30, 33), [M1, k1] twice, M1, k- (-, 22, 25, 29, 29, 33), M1, k1 — - (-, 53, 60, 67, 68, 75) sts. Knit - (-, 0, 0, 1, 1, 1) row(s).

SIZES WOMEN'S LARGE/MEN'S MEDIUM AND MEN'S LARGE ONLY
Increase Row 5: K1, M1, k- (-, -, -, -, 32, 35), [M1, k1] twice, M1, k- (-, -, -, -, 32, 36), M1, k1 — - (-, -, -, -, 73, 80) sts. Don't turn.

ALL SIZES
Next Row: Join for working in the rnd; pm for beginning of rnd. Knit 1 (1, 2, 2, 2, 3, 3) rnd(s).

SIZE CHILD'S SMALL ONLY
Decrease Rnd 1: [K13, k2tog] 3 times, k2—44 sts remain.

SIZES CHILD'S MEDIUM, WOMEN'S MEDIUM/MEN'S SMALL, AND WOMEN'S LARGE/MEN'S MEDIUM ONLY
Decrease Rnd 2: K- (-, 25, - 32, 35, -), k2tog, knit to end— - (-, 52, -, 66, 72, -) sts.

ALL SIZES
Decrease Rnd 3: *K8 (9, 11, 8, 9, 10, 8), k2tog; repeat from * to end—36 (40, 48, 54, 60, 66, 72) sts remain.

Eyelet Rnd: *K2tog, yo; repeat from * to end. BO all sts. Tie piece of non-felting waste yarn in center back eyelet. Fold piece in half widthwise; sew CO edges together, then sew side edges [1].

Felting
Felt Sole well (page 14). While piece is still damp, tug Sole to finished length. Allow to dry [2].

- - - - { BEFORE AND AFTER FELTING } - - - -

[1] Sole before felting.

[2] Sole after felting.

UPPER

Using MC and crochet hook, *insert crochet hook into eyelet, draw up a loop, and place it on dpn [1 and 2]; repeat from * until you have picked up a total of 18 (20, 24, 27, 30, 33, 36) sts on 4 dpns.

Next Rnd: *K1-f/b; repeat from * to end—36 (40, 48, 54, 60, 66, 72) sts. Knit 1 rnd.

Instep Flap

Next Rnd: K14 (16, 20, 22, 25, 27, 30), k2tog, k4 (4, 4, 6, 6, 8, 8), k2tog, slip 1 st, turn—34 (38, 46, 52, 58, 64, 70) sts remain.

Row 1 (WS): P2tog, p4 (4, 4, 6, 6, 8, 8), p2tog, slip 1 st, turn—32 (36, 44, 50, 56, 62, 68) sts remain.

Row 2 (RS): K2tog, k5 (5, 5, 7, 7, 9, 9), k2tog, slip 1 st, turn—30 (34, 42, 48, 54, 60, 66) sts remain.

Row 3: P2tog, p6 (6, 6, 8, 8, 10, 10), p2tog, slip 1 st,

- - - - - - - { STARTING UPPER } - - - - - - -

[1] Insert crochet hook into eyelet, at beginning of rnd, draw up a loop, and place it on dpn.

[2] Continue using crochet hook to place sts on dpns until you reach marker at beginning of rnd.

turn—28 (32, 40, 46, 52, 58, 64) sts remain.

Row 4: K2tog, k6 (6, 6, 8, 8, 10,10), k2tog, slip 1 st, turn—26 (30, 38, 44, 50, 56, 62) sts remain.

Repeat Rows 3 and 4 one (2, 3, 4, 5, 6, 7) time(s), then Row 3 zero (0, 1, 1, 0, 1, 1) time(s), omitting slip 1 on final row—22 (22, 24, 26, 30, 30, 32) sts remain.

SIZES CHILD'S X-SMALL AND WOMEN'S MEDIUM/MEN'S SMALL ONLY

Repeat Row 3 once—20 (-, -, -, 28, -, -) sts remain.

Next Row (RS): K2tog, k6 (-, -, -, 8, -, -), k2tog 18 (-, -, -, 26, -, -) sts remain. Do not turn.

ALL SIZES

Knit to end, closing gap between decreased sts and adjacent sts as follows: When gap is before decreased st, pick up st below decreased st, place it on left-hand needle, and knit it together with decreased st; when gap is after decreased st, slip decreased st to right-hand needle, pick up st below next st and place it on left-hand needle, slip decreased st back to left-hand needle, and knit these 2 sts together.

LEG

Next Rnd: Join for working in the rnd; pm for beginning of rnd. Knit 11 (11, 15, 19, 19, 23, 23) rnds (Leg should measure approximately 3 (3, 4, 5, 5, 6, 6)" [7.5 (7.5, 10, 12.5, 12.5, 15, 15) cm]).

SIZES CHILD'S X-SMALL, CHILD'S SMALL, CHILD'S LARGE/WOMEN'S SMALL, WOMEN'S MEDIUM/MEN'S SMALL, WOMEN'S LARGE/MEN'S MEDIUM, AND WOMEN'S LARGE/MEN'S MEDIUM ONLY

Decrease Rnd: K4 (5, , 6, 6, 7, -) k2tog, k7 (8, -, 10, 10, 12, -), k2tog, k3 (5, -, 6, 6, 7, -)— 16 (20, -, 24, 24, 28, -) sts remain.

ALL SIZES

Change to 2x2 Rib; work even for 4 (4, 4, 6, 6, 8, 8) rnds. BO all sts in pattern.

FINISHING

Soling and Lining

Add soling (see page 18) and lining (see page 22) of your choice. I chose sheepskin lining and Plasti Dip soling for my Boots.

Memories of the white beaded leather moccasins I coveted as a child inspired these filted, sturdy, shoelike slippers. Wear them for a stroll out to the garden or maybe even to the coffee shop. They are shown above with their "cousins," the Ankle Fringe Boots (see page 119).

SIZES
Women's Small (Medium, Large)

FINISHED MEASUREMENTS
11 3/4 (13 1/2, 14 1/4)" [30 (34.5, 36) cm] Foot length, before felting
9 (10, 11)" [23 (25.5, 28) cm] Foot length, after felting

YARN
Ella Rae Classic Wool [100% wool; 220 yards (201 meters / 100 grams]: 1 (1, 2) skein(s) #107 Orange Heather

NEEDLES
One set of five double-pointed needles (dpn) size US 10 1/2 (6.5 mm); change needle size if necessary to obtain correct gauge

NOTIONS
Crochet hook size US K/10 1/2 (6.5 mm), or smaller; newsprint; disposable razor; 18 size 4.5 mm glass beads each in light blue, orange, yellow, white, black, and red; sewing needle; embroidery floss or thread

GAUGE
14 sts and 18 rows = 4" (10 cm) in Stockinette stitch (St st), before felting

OVERVIEW

The Sole is worked back and forth, with increases for the Toe and Heel, then the stitches on the needle are joined and the Upper is worked in the round, with short-row Heel shaping and decreases to shape the Toe. The remaining Toe stitches are left on hold, while the cast-on edge is folded in half and the cast-on and side edges are sewn together, then the Tongue and Fringe are worked from the remaining Toe stitches.

SOLE

CO 53 (59, 65) sts.

Shape Sole

Row 1 and All RS Rows (RS): Knit.
Row 2: K1, M1, k25 (28, 31), M1, k1-f/b, M1, k25 (28, 31), M1, k1 —58 (64, 70) sts.
Row 4: K1, M1, k27 (30, 33), [M1, k1] twice, M1, k27 (30, 33), M1, k1 —63 (69, 75) sts.
Row 6: K1, M1, k30 (33, 36), M1, k1-f/b, M1, k30 (33, 36), M1, k1 —68 (74, 80) sts.
Row 8: K1, M1, k32 (35, 38), [M1, k1] twice, M1, k32 (35, 38), M1, k1 —73 (79, 85) sts.
Row 10: K1, M1, k35 (38, 41), M1, k1-f/b, M1, k35 (38, 41), M1, k1 —78 (84, 90) sts.
Row 12: K1, M1, k37 (40, 43), [M1, k1] twice, M1, k37 (40, 43), M1, k1 —83 (89, 95) sts.
Row 13: Knit.

SIZES MEDIUM AND LARGE ONLY

Row 14: K1, M1, k- (43, 46), M1, k1-f/b, M1, k- (43, 46), M1, k1 — - (94, 100) sts.
Row 15: Knit.

SIZE LARGE ONLY

Row 16: K1, M1, k48, M1, k1, M1, k1, M1, k48, M1, k1 —105 sts.
Row 17: Knit. Do not turn.

UPPER

ALL SIZES

Join for working in the rnd; pm for beginning of rnd. Knit 4 (5, 6) rnds.

Shape Upper

Decrease Rnd: Decrease 2 sts this rnd, then every other rnd 2 (3, 3) times, as follows: K2, k2tog, knit to last 4 sts, ssk, k2—77 (86, 97) sts remain. Knit 1 (0, 0) rnd(s).

HEEL

Note: Heel is shaped using short rows (see Special Techniques, page 152); work wraps together with wrapped sts as you come to them.

Short Row 1 (RS): K9, wrp-t.
Short Row 2 (WS): P18, wrp-t.
Short Row 3: K17, wrp-t.
Short Row 4: P16, wrp-t.
Short Row 5: K15, wrp-t.
Short Row 6: P5, p2tog, sm, p2tog, p5, wrp-t—75 (84, 95) sts remain.

SIZES SMALL AND LARGE ONLY

Short Row 7: K5, k2tog, pm for new beginning of round—74 (-, 94) sts remain. Do not turn.

SIZE MEDIUM ONLY

Short Row 7: K6, pm for new beginning of rnd. Do not turn.

TOE

Set-Up Row (RS): K31 (35, 39), k2tog, k9 (11, 13), k2tog, slip 1 st, turn.
Row 1: P2tog, p10 (12, 14), p2tog, slip 1 st, turn.
Row 2: K2tog, k10 (12, 14), k2tog, slip 1 st, turn.
Repeat Rows 1 and 2 until 48 (54, 60) sts remain. Place marker 18 (20, 22) sts in from each edge.
Decrease Row (RS): [K7 (8, 9), k2tog] twice, k12 (14, 16), [k2tog, k7 (8, 9)] twice—44 (50, 56) sts remain.
Bind-Off Row: BO 16 (18, 20) sts, knit to last 16 (18, 20) sts, BO to end—12 (14, 16) sts remain. Cut yarn, leaving sts on needle. Fold piece in half widthwise; sew CO edges together; then sew sides edges.

TONGUE

With WS facing, rejoin yarn to sts on needle. Continuing in St st, work even for 8 rows. BO all sts.

FINISHING

Fringe

Cut approximately 13 lengths of yarn 6" [15 cm] long. Fold strand in half; with WS of Tongue facing, insert crochet hook just above edge to pull fringe from back to front; catch folded strand of yarn with hook and pull through work to form a loop [1]; insert ends of yarn through loop and pull to tighten [2].

Felting

Felt Moccasins (see page 14). While piece is still damp, stuff with newsprint to shape. Round toe into a pleasing shape and tug Sole to finished length. Pull Fringe into place and smooth down. Trim ends evenly [3]. To remove excess fuzz, shave piece with disposable razor. Allow to dry thoroughly.

[1] Catch folded strand of yarn with hook and pull through work to form a loop.

[2] Insert end of yarn through loop and pull to tighten.

[3] Trim ends of fringe evenly.

{ EMBELLISHING WITH BEADS }

[1] To begin, bring needle up from inside of Moccasin, through 2 layers of felted fabric to top side of Tongue, then slide 3 beads onto needle.

[2] Place each new stack of beads right next to the one before it

Beading

Working with doubled strand of embroidery floss or thread, tie knot in thread. *Note: Refer to photos for bead color sequence.* Beginning approximately 1/8" (.3 cm) in from side edge of Tongue and 1/4" (.5 cm) down from folded edge of Tongue, bring needle up from inside of Moccasin, through 2 layers of felted fabric to top side of Tongue, and slide 3 beads onto needle [1]. Take needle back down to inside of Moccasin, making sure beads lie flat against Tongue. Bring needle back to top side again in original position, back though beads, then to inside again to secure the beads in place. Work in this manner, placing each stack of beads right next to previous stack [2], until you are 1/8" (.3 cm) from opposite side edge of Tongue. Secure thread well inside Moccasin; cut thread.

Soling and Lining

Add soling (see page 18) and lining (see page 22) of your choice.

I lined mine with wool felt and sewed on a leather sole. I also embroidered a feather onto my lining, which you can see in the photo on page 2.

These sweet baby booties are an easy project for a beginner knitter and an especially quick project for an experienced knitter. Because garter stitch is stretchy, these booties will fit a growing baby for a long time. The tie cord keeps them in place on baby's feet.

SIZES
0-3 (3-6, 6-12, 12-18) months

FINISHED MEASUREMENTS
3 1/2 (4, 4 1/2, 5)" [9 (10, 11, 12.5) cm] Foot length

YARN
Malabrigo Arroyo [100% wool; 335 yards (306 meters) / 100 grams]: 1 hank #856 Azules

NEEDLES
One set of five double-pointed needles (dpn) size US 3 (3.25 mm); change needle size if necessary to obtain correct gauge

NOTIONS
Stitch markers

GAUGE
24 sts and 48 rows = 4" (10 cm) in Garter stitch

OVERVIEW
The Cuff is worked back and forth, with an eyelet row for the Ties, then the stitches are rearranged on the needles and the Foot is worked in the round, with Foot and Sole shaping. The sides of the Sole are joined using Three-Needle Bind-Off, then I-Cord Ties are worked and threaded through the eyelets.

CUFF
CO 30 (32, 36, 40) sts. Knit 14 (16, 18, 20) rows.
Eyelet Row (RS): K4 (2, 4, 3), *yo, k2tog, k1; repeat from * to last 2 (0, 2, 1) st(s), k2 (0, 2, 1). Knit 1 row. Break yarn.

FOOT
Divide sts among 4 needles [7-8-7-8 (8-8-8-8, 9-9-9-9, 10-10-10-10)]. With RS facing, rejoin yarn to center of piece, between center 2 needles. K 15 (16, 18, 20), join for working in the rnd, k 15 (16, 18, 20); pm for beginning of rnd.

Shape Foot
Increase Rnd 1: P 12 (13, 15, 17), p1-f/b, pm, p4, pm, p1-f/b, p 12 (13, 15, 17)—32 (34, 38, 42) sts.
Increase Rnd 2: Knit to 1 st before marker, k1-f/b, sm, knit to marker, sm, k1-f/b, knit to end—34 (36, 40, 44) sts.
Increase Rnd 3: Purl to 1st before marker, p1-f/b, sm, purl to marker, sm, p1-f/b, purl to end—36 (38, 42, 46) sts.
Repeat Increase Rnds 2 and 3 four (4, 5, 5) times, then Increase Rnd 2 zero (1, 0, 1) time(s)—52 (56, 62, 68) sts.
Continuing in Garter st as established, work even for 4 (5, 6, 7) rnds.

SOLE
Shape Sole
Decrease Rnd 1: K1, k2tog, knit to 2 sts before marker, k2tog, remove marker, k2, pm, k2, remove marker, k2tog, knit to last 3 sts, k2tog, k1—48 (52, 58, 64) sts remain. Purl 1 rnd.
Decrease Rnd 2: K1, k2tog, knit to 2 sts before marker, k2tog, sm, k2, sm, k2tog, knit to last 3 sts k2tog, k1—44 (48, 54, 60) sts remain. Purl 1 rnd.
Repeat Decrease Rnd 2 every other rnd 3 (3, 5, 5) times—32 (36, 34, 40) sts remain.

FINISHING
Slip sts from second needle onto first needle, and sts from fourth needle onto third needle. With RSs together, using 3-Needle BO (see Special Techniques, page 152), working p2tog instead of k2tog, and working into first st on back needle, then first st on front needle, BO all sts.

I-CORD TIES (Make 2)
CO 2 sts. Work I-Cord (see Special Techniques, page 151) 7" (18 cm) long. Thread I-Cord through Eyelet Row.

These squishy socks are my nod to the 1980s. Loose, generous ribbing tops a thick, dense sock, perfect for weekend lounging. They are worked from the top down, with larger needles for the ribbing and smaller needles for the foot.

SIZES
Women's Small (Medium, Large)

FINISHED MEASUREMENTS
7 1/4 (8, 8 3/4)" [18.5 (20.5, 22) cm] Foot circumference
9 (10, 11)" [23 (25.5, 28) cm] Foot length

YARN
Queensland Collection Kathmandu Chunky [85% wool / 10% silk / 5% cashmere; 142 yards (130 meters) / 100 grams]: 2 (2, 3) balls #113 Green

NEEDLES
One set of five double-pointed needles (dpn) size US 8 (5 mm); one set of five double-pointed needles size US 4 (3.5 mm); change needle size if necessary to obtain correct gauge

NOTIONS
Stitch marker

GAUGE
20 sts and 28 rows = 4" (10 cm) in Stockinette stitch (St st), using smaller needles

OVERVIEW

The Cuff is worked in the round, then the Heel Flap is shaped using short rows. The Foot and shaped Toe are worked in the round, and the Toe is grafted using Kitchener stitch.

STITCH PATTERN

1x1 Rib
(multiple of 2 sts; 1-rnd repeat)
All Rnds: *K1, p1; repeat from * to end.

CUFF

Using larger needles, CO 36 (40, 44). Divide sts among 4 dpns. Join for working in the rnd, being careful not to twist sts; pm for beginning of rnd. Begin 1x1 Rib; work even until piece measures 8 (9, 10)" [20.5 (23, 25.5) cm] from the beginning. Change to smaller needles; work even for 1" (2.5 cm). Knit 1 rnd.

HEEL

Note: Heel is shaped using short rows (see Special Techniques, page 152); work wraps together with wrapped sts as you come to them.
Set-Up Row (RS): K9 (10, 11), place last 18 (20, 22) sts worked on one needle, turn.
Short Row 1 (WS): P17 (19, 21), wrp-t.
Short Row 2: K16 (18, 20), wrp-t.
Short Rows 3-12: Continuing in St st, work 1 less st on each row before working wrp-t, until there are 6 (8, 10) sts remaining between wraps, and there are 6 wraps on each side.
Short Row 13: P7 (9, 11), wrp-t.
Short Row 14: K8 (10, 12), wrp-t.
Short Rows 15-21: Continue working 1 more st on each row before working wrp-t, until you have 15 (17, 19) sts between wraps.
Short Row 22: K8 (9, 10), pm for new beginning of rnd.

FOOT

Rejoin for working in the rnd; continuing in St st, work even until piece measures 7 3/4 (8, 8 1/4)" [19.5 (20.5, 21) cm], or to 1 1/4 (2, 2 3/4)" [3 (5, 7) cm] less than desired length from back of Heel.

TOE

SIZE MEDIUM ONLY

Decrease Rnd 1: K9, k2tog, k18, ssk, k9—38 sts remain. Knit 1 rnd.
Decrease Rnd 2: K8, k2tog, k18, ssk, k8—36 sts remain. Knit 1 rnd.

SIZE LARGE ONLY

Decrease Rnd 3: [K8, k2tog, k2, ssk, k8] twice—40 sts remain. Knit 1 rnd.
Decrease Rnd 4: [K7, k2tog, k2, ssk, k7] twice—36 sts remain. Knit 1 rnd.

ALL SIZES

Decrease Rnd 5: [K6, k2tog, k2, ssk, k6] twice—32 sts remain. Knit 1 rnd.
Decrease Rnd 6: [K5, k2tog, k2, ssk, k5] twice—28 sts remain. Knit 1 rnd.
Decrease Rnd 7: [K4, k2tog, k2, ssk, k4] twice—24 sts remain. Knit 1 rnd.
Decrease Rnd 8: [K3, k2tog, k2, ssk, k3] twice—20 sts remain. Knit 1 rnd.
Decrease Rnd 9: [K2, k2tog, k2, ssk, k2] twice—16 sts remain. Knit 1 rnd.

FINISHING

Cut yarn, leaving a long tail. K4, place last 8 sts worked on one needle and remaining 8 sts on a second needle. Using Kitchener st (see Special Techniques, page 151), graft Toe sts.

For guaranteed comfort, I work the sole of these children's slipper socks in reverse Stockinette stitch, so the smooth side of the stitches touch the skin and the potentially less cozy purl bumps are on the outside. The ribbing on the leg and across the top of the foot make for a very flexible fit.

SIZES
Child's Small (Medium, Large)

FINISHED MEASUREMENTS
7 (8, 9)" [18 (20.5, 23) cm] Foot length

YARN
Cascade Yarns Cascade 220 [100% Peruvian Highland wool; 220 yards (201 meters) / 100 grams]: 1 hank #9544 Midnight Sun

NEEDLES
One set of five double-pointed needles (dpn) size US 3 (3.25 mm); change needle size if necessary to obtain correct gauge

NOTIONS
Stitch marker; piece of suede large enough for 2 soles; double-stick tape; leather needle; embroidering floss or heavy-duty thread to match yarn

GAUGE
18 sts and 28 rows = 4" (10 cm) in Stockinette stitch (St st)

STITCH PATTERN
3x3 Rib
(multiple of 6 sts; 1-rnd repeat)
All Rnds: *K3, p3; repeat from * to end.

OVERVIEW

The Leg is worked in the round, and the Heel is shaped using short rows. The Gusset, Foot, and shaped Toe are worked in reverse Stockinette stitch in the round, then the Toe is joined using Kitchener stitch.

LEG

CO 42 sts. Divide sts among 4 needles. Join for working in the rnd, being careful not to twist sts; pm for beginning of rnd. Begin 3x3 Rib; work even until piece measures 5½ (6, 7)" [14 (15, 18 cm)] from the beginning.

HEEL FLAP

Set-Up Row 1 (RS): Continuing in 3x3 Rib, work 21 sts, turn.
Set-Up Row 2: Slip 1, work 20 sts, working all 21 sts onto 1 needle for Heel Flap and removing marker. Leave remaining 21 sts on 2 needles for instep.
Working on 21 Heel Flap sts only, work even for 10 rows, slipping the first st of every row.

TURN HEEL

Set-Up Row 1 (RS): P 11, p2tog, p 1, turn—20 sts remain.
Set-Up Row 2: Slip 1, k4, ssk, k 1, turn—19 sts remain.
Row 1: Slip 1, purl to 1 st before gap, p2tog (the 2 sts on either side of gap), p 1, turn—18 sts remain.
Row 2: Slip 1, knit to 1 st before gap, k2tog (the 2 sts on either side of gap), k 1, turn—17 sts remain.
Repeat Rows 1 and 2 twice, then Row 1 once, omitting final k 1 and p 1 on last 2 rows—12 sts remain.

GUSSET

Continuing to work with RS facing, pick up and knit 6 sts, picking up sts from slipped Heel Flap sts, work 21 sts in 3x3 Rib as established, pick up and knit 6 sts from slipped Heel Flap sts, p6—45 sts. Join for working in the rnd; pm for beginning of rnd.
Next Rnd: P 10, p2tog, work 21 sts in 3x3 Rib, p2tog, p 10—43 sts remain.
Next Rnd: P9, p2tog, work 21 sts in 3x3 Rib, p2tog, p9—41 sts remain.

FOOT

Work even in patterns as established until piece measures 5½ (6½, 7½)" [14 (16.5, 19) cm], or 1½" (4 cm) less than desired length from back of Heel. Place markers 10 sts to either side of beginning-of-rnd marker.

TOE

Decrease Rnd 1: [Work to 3 sts before marker, p2tog, p 1, sm, p 1, p2tog] twice, work to end—37 sts remain. Work even for 1 rnd.
Repeat Decrease Rnd 1 every other rnd 4 times—21 sts remain. Work even for 1 rnd, removing second and third markers.
Decrease Rnd 2: [P2, p2tog] twice, p 1, k 1, skp, p 1, [p2tog, p2] twice—16 sts remain. Work even for 1 rnd.
Decrease Rnd 3: P 1, p2tog, p3, p2tog, skp, p3, p2tog, p 1, p3 from next rnd—12 sts remain.

FINISHING

Cut yarn, leaving a long tail. Rearrange sts so that next 6 sts are on one needle and last 6 sts worked are on second needle. Turn sock inside out. Using Kitchener st (see Special Techniques, page 151), graft Toe sts.

Soling

Add soling of your choice (see page 18). I used a sewn-on suede sole for mine.

These ladies' flats are quick to knit (I finished a pair in an evening) and easy to customize. The pattern includes instructions for an over-sized pom-pom, felted bow, and needle-felted flowers; you might want to experiment with ribbon, beads, or other trims as well.

SIZES
Women's Small (Medium, Large)

FINISHED MEASUREMENTS
11 (12, 14)" [28 (30.5, 35.5) cm] Foot length, before felting
9 (10, 11)" [23 (25.5, 28) cm] Foot length, after felting

YARN
Brown Sheep Lamb's Pride Worsted [85% wool / 15% mohair; 190 yards (173 meters) / 4 ounces (114 grams)]: 1 skein #M14 Sunburst Gold, #M160 Dynamite Blue, or #M18 Khaki

NEEDLES
One set of five double-pointed needles (dpn) size US 10½ (6.5 mm); change needle size if necessary to obtain correct gauge

NOTIONS
Crochet hook size US K/10½ (6.5 mm), or one size larger; waste yarn; stitch marker; disposable razor

For Bow (optional): Sewing needle and matching thread
For Pom-Pom (optional): Approximately 40 yards (36.5 meters) worsted weight yarn; sewing needle and matching thread
For Needle Felting (optional): Needle felting needles; bubble wrap with small bubbles, or needle felting foam; Peace Fleece wool batting in dark pink, light pink, light green, dark green, and brown (all available in their Rainbow Felting Pack)

GAUGE
14 sts and 18 rows = 4" (10 cm) in Stockinette stitch (St st), before felting

OVERVIEW

The Flats are worked from the Toe up, beginning with a provisional cast-on and shaping the Toe using short rows. The Foot is picked up from the provisional cast-on and worked back and forth to the Heel, which is shaped using short rows. An I-Cord Edging is worked around the Foot opening to give structure to the edges. The Flats are felted, then embellished with your choice of trim.

TOE

Using crochet hook, waste yarn, and Provisional CO (see Special Techniques, page 152), CO 16 (18, 20) sts. Change to dpns and color of your choice.

Shape Toe

Note: Toe is shaped using short rows (see Special Techniques, page 152); work wraps together with wrapped sts as you come to them.

Short Row 1 (RS): K 15 (17, 19), wrp-t.
Short Row 2: P 14 (16, 18), wrp-t.
Short Row 3: K 13 (15, 17), wrp-t.
Short Row 4: P 12 (14, 16), wrp-t.
Short Row 5: K 11 (13, 15), wrp-t.
Short Row 6: P 10 (12, 14), wrp-t.
Short Row 7: K 9 (11, 13), wrp-t.
Short Row 8: P 8 (10, 12), wrp-t.

SIZES MEDIUM AND LARGE ONLY

Short Row 9: K- (9, 11), wrp-t.
Short Row 10: P- (8, 10), wrp-t.

SIZE LARGE ONLY

Short Row 11: K 9, wrp-t.
Short Row 12: P 8, wrp-t.

ALL SIZES

Short Row 13: K 9, wrp-t.
Short Row 14: P 10, wrp-t.
Short Row 15: K 11, wrp-t.

Short Row 16: P 12, wrp-t.
Short Row 17: K 13, wrp-t.
Short Row 18: P 14, wrp-t.

SIZES MEDIUM AND LARGE ONLY

Short Row 19: K 15, wrp-t.
Short Row 20: P 16, wrp-t.

SIZE LARGE ONLY

Short Row 21: K 17, wrp-t.
Short Row 22: P 18, wrp-t.

ALL SIZES

Carefully unpick Provisional CO and place sts on spare dpn. Knit to end, knit across sts from Provisional CO—32 (36, 40) sts. Join for working in the rnd; pm for beginning of rnd. Knit 4 rnds.

Bind-Off Row (RS): K2 (3, 4), BO next 12 sts, knit to end, k2 (3, 4) from beginning of next rnd, removing marker—
20 (24, 28) sts remain.

FOOT

Working back and forth in St st, work even for 11 (11, 13) rows.

Shape Foot

Increase Row (RS): K 1, k 1-f/b, knit to last 2 sts, k 1-f/b, k 1—22 (26, 30) sts. Work even for 9 (9, 11) rows.
Repeat Increase Row once—24 (28, 32) sts. Work even for 9 (9, 11) rows.

HEEL

Note: Heel is shaped using short rows; work wraps to-gether with wrapped sts as you come to them.
Short Row 1 (RS): K19 (22, 25), wrp-t.
Short Row 2: P14 (16, 18), wrp-t.
Short Row 3: K13 (15, 17), wrp-t.
Short Row 4: P12 (14, 16), wrp-t.
Short Row 5: K11 (13, 15), wrp-t.
Short Row 6: P10 (12, 14), wrp-t.
Short Row 7: K9 (11, 13), wrp-t.
Short Row 8: P8 (10, 12), wrp-t.

SIZES MEDIUM AND LARGE ONLY
Short Row 9: K- (9, 11), wrp-t.
Short Row 10: P- (8, 10), wrp-t.

SIZE LARGE ONLY
Short Row 11: K9, wrp-t.
Short Row 12: P8, wrp-t.

ALL SIZES
Short Row 13: K9, wrp-t.
Short Row 14: P10, wrp-t.
Short Row 15: K11, wrp-t.
Short Row 16: P12, wrp-t.
Short Row 17: K13, wrp-t.
Short Row 18: P14, wrp-t.

SIZES MEDIUM AND LARGE ONLY
Short Row 19: K15, wrp-t.
Short Row 20: P16, wrp-t.

SIZE LARGE ONLY
Short Row 21: K17 wrp-t.
Short Row 22: P18 wrp-t.

ALL SIZES
Short Row 23: Knit to end. Purl 1 row.
Short Row 24: K19 (22, 25), k2tog, wrp-t—23 (27, 31) sts remain.
Short Row 25: P15 (17, 19), p2tog-tbl, wrp-t—22 (26, 30) sts remain.
Short Row 26: K15 (17, 19), k2tog, wrp-t—21 (25, 29) sts remain.
Repeat Short Rows 25 and 26 one (2, 3) time(s)—19 (21, 23) sts remain.
Short Row 27: Purl to end.
Decrease Row 1 (RS): K1, k2tog, k5 (6, 7), k2tog, k6 (7, 8), k2tog, k1—16 (18, 20) sts remain.
Decrease Row 2 (RS): P1, p2tog, p4 (5, 6), p2tog, p4 (5, 6), p2tog, p1—13 (15, 17) sts remain.
Decrease Row 3 (RS): K1, k2tog, k3 (4, 5), k2tog, k2 (3, 4), k2tog, k1, pick up and knit 16 (18, 20) sts along side edge of Foot, 6 (8, 10) sts from Toe, then 16 (18, 20) sts along second side edge of Foot—48 (56, 64) sts. Do not turn.

Attached I-Cord Edging
Using Backward Loop CO (see Special Techniques, page 151), CO 3 sts. K2, k2tog-tbl (last st from I-Cord together with 1 st from top edge of Slipper); *slide sts back to right-hand end of dpn; using empty dpn, working sts from right to left, and pulling yarn from left to right for first st, k2, k2tog-tbl (last st from I-Cord together with 1 st from top edge of Slipper); repeat from * around entire top edge of Foot until 3 sts remain. BO off all sts. Sew BO edge to CO edge.

FINISHING

Felt Flats well (see page 14). While damp, stuff with newsprint to form. Round toe into a pleasing shape and tug Sole to finished length. Remove excess fuzz with disposable razor. Dry thoroughly.

Soling

Add soling of your choice (see page 18). I used a sewn-on suede sole for mine.

Bow

Using color of your choice, CO 9 sts. Begin St st, beginning with a purl row; work even for 11 rows.

Shape Bow

Decrease Row (RS): Continuing in St st, decrease 2 sts this row, then every other row once, as follows: K 1, k2tog, knit to last 3 sts, k2tog, k1—5 sts remain. Work even for 9 rows.
Increase Row (RS): Increase 1 st this row, then every other row once, as follows: K 1, k1-f/b, knit to last 2 sts, k1-f/b, k1—9 sts. Work even for 10 rows. BO all sts.

Felt piece well, then remove excess fuzz with disposable razor. Dry thoroughly. Tie in knot to form bow [1]. Sew to Toe (see photo).

Pom-Pom

Using color of your choice, wrap yarn around your fingers approximately 100 times [2]. Cut yarn. Cut 1 strand in matching color 12" (30.5 cm) long; tie tightly around center of wraps [3]. Trim ends of Pom-Pom, leaving long tail [4]. Using tail, sew to Slipper [5].

- - - - - { MAKING BOWS } - - - - -

[1] After bows have dried, tie a knot in the center of each.

- - - - { MAKING POM-POMS } - - - -

[2] To begin Pom-Pom, wrap yarn around your fingers approximately 100 times.

[3] Tightly tie 12" (30.5 cm) strand around center.

[4] Trim ends of Pom-Pom, leaving tail long.

[5] Using tail, sew Pom-Pom to Slipper.

Needle Felting

Roll bubble wrap into a cylinder and secure with rubber bands to use as a work surface. Following template, needle felt details onto Slipper (see Special Techniques, page 151). For branch, twist thin piece of brown batting into rope shape and needle felt it onto Flat [1]. For flower, needle felt large circle of light pink batting, then needle felt dark pink center on top of light pink circle. For leaf, needle felt whole leaf from light green batting, then add darker shading to half of leaf [2].

{ NEEDLE FELTING }

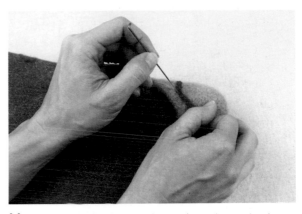

[1] For branch, twist thin piece of brown batting into rope shape and needle felt it onto Flat.

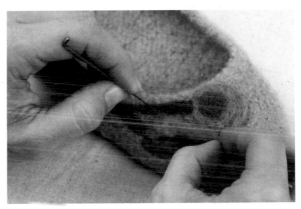

[2] Needle felt entire leaf with light green batting, then add dark green shading to half of Leaf.

{ FLOWER TEMPLATE }

Enlarge template by 286%

Made with luxurious suri alpaca yarn, these minimalist slippers are meant for serious lounging and comfort. If you want to do a lot of walking in them, I suggest adding a sewn-on suede sole.

SIZES
Women's Small (Medium, Large)

FINISHED MEASUREMENTS
8½ (9½, 10½)" [21.5 (24, 26.5) cm] Foot length
Note: Slip-ons are intended to be worn with ½" [1.5 cm] negative ease.

YARN
Blue Sky Alpacas Brushed Suri [67% baby suri alpaca / 22% merino wool / 11% bamboo; 142 yards (130 meters) / 50 grams]: 2 hanks #908 Snow Cone

NEEDLES
One pair straight needles size US 8 (5 mm); change needle size if necessary to obtain correct gauge

GAUGE
15 sts and 20 rows = 4" (10 cm) in Stockinette stitch (St st)

OVERVIEW
The Body is worked back and forth until it is approximately twice the length of the Foot. Four Sole pieces (two for each Slip-On) are worked back and forth, then each pair is sewn together to create a two-layer Sole. The Upper is sewn to the Sole, overlapping the excess fabric at the Toe.

BODY
Cast on 19 (22, 25) sts. Begin St st; work even until piece measures 19 (21, 23)" [48.5 (53.5, 58.5) cm] from the beginning, ending with a WS row. BO all sts.

SOLE (make 4)
Cast on 7 (9, 9) sts. Knit 1 row.

Shape Sole
Increase Row (WS): Increase 2 sts this row, then every other row once, as follows: P2, M1-p, purl to last 2 sts, M1-p, p2—11 (13, 13) sts.
Continuing in St st, work even until piece measures 7½ (8½, 9½)" [19 (21.5, 24) cm] from the beginning, ending with a WS row.
Decrease Row (RS): Decrease 2 sts this row, then every other row once, as follows: K2, k2tog, knit to last 4 sts, k2tog, k2—7 (9, 9) sts remain. BO all sts.

FINISHING
With WSs together and using small whip sts, sew Sole pieces together. Fold Body in half lengthwise, with WSs together. Pin to Sole, overlapping excess fabric at Toe. Using small whip sts, sew to Sole. Tack pieces together where they cross on top of foot. *Note: Be sure to overlap second slipper to mirror the first.*

Leather tassels top these simple menswear-inspired but unisex loafers. Worked in chunky yarn, they are quick to knit.

SIZES
Child's Large/Women's Small (Women's Medium/ Men's Small, Women's Large/Men's Medium, Men's Large)

FINISHED MEASUREMENTS
8 (9, 10, 11)" [20.5 (23, 25.5, 28) cm] Foot length.
Note: Loafers are intended to be worn with approximately 1" (2.5 cm) of negative ease.

YARN
Worsted Peace Fleece [75% wool / 25% mohair; 200 yards (183 meters) / 4 ounces (114 grams)]: 1 (1, 2, 2) hank(s) Blue Jay

NEEDLES
One set of five double-pointed needles (dpn) size US 10½ (6.5 mm); change needle size if necessary to obtain correct gauge

NOTIONS
Stitch marker; 4½ yards (4 meters) of ⅛" (.3 cm) wide leather lace; embroidery floss or heavy thread to match yarn; embroidery or large eye sewing needle

GAUGE
13 sts and 16 rows = 4" (10 cm) in Stockinette stitch (St st), using 2 strands of yarn held together

OVERVIEW

The Loafers begin with the Heel Flap, then the Sole, both of which are worked back and forth. Stitches are picked up from the Heel Flap and Sole for the Upper, then the Upper is joined and worked in the round, using short rows for shaping. Stitches are bound off for the foot opening, then the Tongue is worked back and forth from the remaining stitches, and the side edges of the Heel Flap are sewn to the Upper.

HEEL FLAP

Using 2 strands of yarn held together, CO 6 (6, 8, 8) sts. Begin St st, beginning with a knit row; work even for 12 (12, 14, 14) rows, slipping the first st of every row.

SOLE

Shape Sole

Increase Row (RS): Continuing in St st, slipping the first st of every row, increase 2 sts this row, then every other row 1 (1, 2, 2) time(s), as follows: Slip 1, M1, knit to last st, M1, k1—10 (10, 14, 14) sts. Work even for 30 (34, 36, 40) rows.

Decrease Row (RS): Continuing in St st, slipping the first st of every row, decrease 2 sts this row, then every other row 1 (1, 2, 2) time(s), as follows: Slip 1, k2tog, knit to last 3 sts, ssk, k1—6 (6, 8, 8) sts remain. BO all sts.

UPPER

Note: The first and last 3 (3, 4, 4) sts picked up for Upper will be picked up from WS of Heel Flap; the remaining sts will be picked up from RS of Sole. To work pick-ups, begin with RS of Sole facing, with Heel Flap at top end of Sole.

Fold Heel Flap to RS so that you are looking at WS of Heel Flap. Beginning at center of Heel Flap, pick up and knit 3 (3, 4, 4) sts from purl bumps of third Heel Flap row above beginning of Sole; with RS of Sole facing, pick up and knit 19 (21, 24, 26) sts along side edge of Sole, 6 (6, 8, 8) sts across BO edge, 19 (21, 24, 26) sts along second side edge of Sole, then with WS of Heel Flap facing, pick up and knit 3 (3, 4, 4) sts to center of Heel Flap—50 (54, 64, 68) sts. Join for working in the rnd; pm for beginning of rnd. Knit 6 (6, 7, 8) rnds.

Shape Upper

Note: Upper is shaped using short rows (see Special Techniques, page 152); work wraps together with wrapped sts as you come to them.

Short Row 1 (RS): K8 (8, 10, 10), wrp-t.

Short Row 2 (WS): P16 (16, 20, 20) (slipping marker), wrp-t.

Short Row 3: K4 (4, 6, 6), k2tog, k2, sm, k2, skp, k3 (3, 5, 5), wrp-t—48 (52, 62, 66) sts remain.

Short Row 4: P12 (12, 14, 14), wrp-t.

Short Row 5: Knit to end.

Knit 1 (1, 2, 2) rnd(s).

Short Row 6: BO 11 (12, 14, 15) sts, k14 (15, 18, 19), skp, k1, wrp-t—36 (39, 47, 50) sts remain.

Short Row 7: Slip 1, p5 (5, 7, 7), p2tog, p1, wrp-t—35 (38, 46, 49) sts remain.

Short Row 8: Slip 1, k6 (6, 8, 8), skp, k1, wrp-t—34 (37, 45, 48) sts remain.

Short Row 9: Slip 1, p7 (7, 9, 9), p2tog, p1, wrp-t—33 (36, 44, 47) sts remain.

Short Row 10: Slip 1, k8 (8, 10, 10), skp, k1, wrp-t—32 (35, 43, 46) sts remain.

Short Row 11: Slip 1, p9 (9, 11, 11), p2tog, p1, wrp-t—31 (34, 42, 45) sts remain.

Short Row 12: Slip 1, k10 (10, 12, 12), skp, k1, wrp-t—30 (33, 41, 44) sts remain.

Short Row 13: Slip 1, p10 (10, 12, 12), p2tog, p1, wrp-t—29 (32, 40, 43) sts remain.

Repeat Short Rows 12 and 13 two (3, 5, 6) times—25 (26, 30, 31) sts remain.

Next Row (RS): BO 2 sts (beginning with wrapped st), k9 (9, 11, 11), BO remaining sts—10 (10, 12, 12) sts remain. Cut yarn.

TONGUE

With RS facing, rejoin yarn to sts on needle. Continuing in St st, slipping the first st of every row, work even for 2 rows.

Decrease Row 1 (RS): Slip 1, k2tog, knit to last 3 sts, k2tog, k1—8 (8, 10, 10) sts remain.

Decrease Row 2 (WS): Slip 1, p2tog, p2 (2, 4, 4), p2tog, p1—6 (6, 8, 8) sts remain. BO all sts.

FINISHING
Sew side edges of Heel Flap to Upper.

Tassels (make 4)
Cut 5 pieces of leather lace 8" (20.5 cm) long for each Tassel. Holding 4 pieces together, fold in half and temporarily tie 15" (38 cm) long piece of embroidery floss around fold. Pin to flat surface [1]. With fifth piece of lace, make a small loop and lay vertically on top of folded strand [2]. Wrap one end of fifth lace tightly around folded strands a few times, working from the top down (be sure to wrap around loop without covering completely as well), then pull tightly through loop [3].

Thread remaining end of fifth lace on a yarn needle and pull through wraps. Trim all ends evenly. Remove embroidery floss from first Tassel. Make 3 more Tassels the same way. Using embroidery floss, sew 2 Tassels to Tongue, making sure to tie knot on WS to secure Tassels [4].

- { MAKING TASSELS } -

[1] Pin 4 strands of leather lacing tied with embroidery floss to flat work surface.

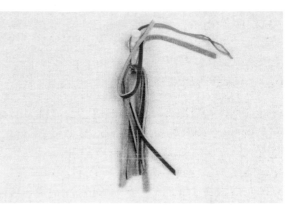

[2] With fifth piece of lace, make a small loop and lay vertically on top of folded strands.

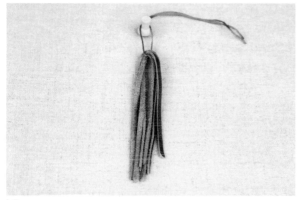

[3] Wrap one end of lacing tightly around folded strands a few times and then pull tightly through loop.

[4] Thread floss through both tassels and use it to sew them to Tongue.

Needle-felted paisleys, beads, and sequins add to the exotic Arabian style of these curly-toed slip-ons.

SIZES
Women's Small (Medium, Large)

FINISHED MEASUREMENTS
8¾ (10, 11¼)" [22 (25.5, 28.5) cm] Foot circumference, before felting
7¾ (9, 10)" [19.5 (23, 25.5) cm] Foot circumference, after felting
12¼ (12½, 14)" [31 (32, 35.5) cm] Foot length, before felting
9½ (10½, 11½)" [24 (26.5, 29) cm] Foot length, after felting

YARN
Brown Sheep Lamb's Pride Worsted [85% wool / 15% mohair; 190 yards (173 meters) / 4 ounces (114 grams)]: 1 (1, 1, 2) skein(s) #M162 Mulberry

NEEDLES
One set of five double-pointed needles (dpn) size US 10½ (6.5 mm); change needle size if necessary to obtain correct gauge

NOTIONS
Stitch marker; disposable razor; beeswax; embroidery floss in yellow; thin cardboard; small amounts of roving in turquoise, lime green, and red; felting needle; bubble wrap with small bubbles; tailor's chalk; size 10/0 glass seed beads in yellow, orange, and clear; 5/16" (8 mm) sequins in pink, clear, and gold; thread or embroidery floss to match beads and sequins; embroidery needle; 12" (30.5 cm) square of suede; paper for Sole pattern

GAUGE
14 sts and 18 rows = 4" (10 cm) in Stockinette stitch (St st), before felting

OVERVIEW

The Slippers are worked back and forth from the Toe up, beginning with I-Cord for the curled Toe. The first half of the Foot is joined and worked in the round, then the second half is worked back and forth with simple shaping. A Footbed is worked to match the shape of the Foot, then the Footbed and Slipper are sewn together. The Slippers are felted, then embellished using embroidery, sequins, and seed beads. A cardboard liner gives them necessary structure.

TOE

CO 1 st. Begin I-Cord (see Special Techniques, page 151).

Shape Toe

Rnd 1 and all Odd-Numbered Rnds: Knit.

Rnd 2: K 1-f/b—2 sts.

Rnd 4: K 1, k 1-f/b—3 sts.

Rnd 6: [K 1-f/b] twice, k 1 —5 sts.

Rnd 8: K 1, [k 1-f/b] twice, k 2—7 sts.

Rnd 10: K 2, k 1-f/b, k 1, k 1-f/b, k 2—9 sts.

Rnd 12: Discontinue I-Cord. Divide sts onto 4 dpns. Join for working in the rnd; pm for beginning of rnd. K 4, k 1-f/b, k 3, k 1-f/b—11 sts.

Rnd 14: K 4, k 1-f/b, k 5, k 1-f/b—13 sts.

Rnd 16: K 6, k 1-f/b, k 5, k 1-f/b—15 sts.

Rnd 18: K 6, k 1-f/b, k 7, k 1-f/b—17 sts.

Rnd 20: K 8, k 1-f/b, k 7, k 1-f/b—19 sts.

Rnd 22: K 8, k 1-f/b, k 9, k 1-f/b—21 sts.

Rnd 24: K 9, k 1-f/b, k 10, k 1-f/b—23 sts.

Rnd 26: K 11, k 1-f/b, k 10, k 1-f/b—25 sts.

Rnd 28: K 11, k 1-f/b, k 12, k 1-f/b—27 sts.

Rnd 30: K 13, k 1-f/b, k 12, k 1-f/b—29 sts.

Rnd 32: K 13, k 1-f/b, k 14, k 1-f/b—31 sts.

Rnd 34: K 15, k 1-f/b, k 14, k 1-f/b—33 sts.

Rnd 36: K 16, k 1-f/b, k 15, k 1-f/b—35 sts.

SIZES MEDIUM AND LARGE ONLY

Rnd 37: Knit.

Rnd 38: K 16, k 1-f/b, k 17, k 1-f/b—37 sts.

Rnd 40: K 18, k 1-f/b, k 17, k 1-f/b—39 sts.

SIZE LARGE ONLY

Rnd 41: Knit.

Rnd 42: K 18, k 1-f/b, K 19, k 1-f/b—41 sts.

Rnd 44: K 20 k 1-f/b, K 19, k 1-f/b—43 sts.

FOOT

ALL SIZES

Knit 12 (11, 10) rnds.

Shape Foot

Decrease Rnd 1: K3 (2, 1), [k2tog, k2 (3, 4)] 3 times, k2tog, k18 (20, 22)—31 (35, 39) sts remain.

Next Row (RS): Change to working back and forth, removing marker. K4 (3, 2), BO next 7 (9, 11) sts, knit past marker to BO sts, removing marker—24 (26, 28) sts remain.

Decrease Row 2 (WS): Slip 1, p2tog, purl to end—23 (25, 27) sts remain.

Decrease Row 3: Slip 1, k2tog, knit to end—22 (24, 26) sts remain.

Repeat Decrease Rows 2 and 3 four times—14 (16, 18) sts remain. Work even in St st for 8 (8, 10) rows.

Decrease Row 4 (WS): Slip 1, p2tog, purl to last 3 sts, p2tog, p1—12 (14, 16) sts remain.

Decrease Row 5: Slip 1, k2tog, knit to last 3 sts, k2tog, k1—10 (12, 14) sts remain.

Repeat Decrease Rows 4 and 5 once, then repeat Decrease Row 1 zero (0, 1) time(s)—6 (8, 8) sts remain. BO all sts.

FOOTBED

CO 6 (8, 8) sts.

Shape Footbed

Increase Row 1 (RS): Slip 1, k1-f/b, knit to last 2 sts, k1-f/b, k1—8 (10, 10) sts.

Increase Row 2: Slip 1, p1-f/b, purl to last 2 sts, p1-f/b, p1—10 (12, 12) sts.

Repeat Increase Rows 1 and 2 once, then repeat Increase Row 1 zero (0, 1) time(s)—14 (16, 18) sts. Work even in St st for 42 (48, 53) rows.

Decrease Row 1: Slip 1, k2tog, knit to last 3 sts, k2tog, k1—12 (14, 16) sts remain.

Decrease Row 2: Slip 1, p2tog, purl to last 3 sts, p2tog, p1—10 (12, 14) sts remain.

Repeat Decrease Rows 1 and 2 once, then repeat Decrease Row 1 zero (0, 1) time(s)—6 (8, 8) sts remain. BO all sts.

FINISHING

Turn Slipper inside out. Lay Footbed on inside bottom of Slipper, with WSs together. Line up narrow end of Footbed with heel of Slipper, centering Footbed on Slipper widthwise. Pin in place, then sew in place with small sts, leaving heel open [1].

Felting

Felt Slippers by hand (see page 14). *Note: I do not recommend machine-felting this project.* After felting, while Slippers are still damp, tack toes temporarily into curled shape and stuff Slippers with newsprint to shape [2]. To remove excess fuzz, shave piece with disposable razor. Allow to dry thoroughly. Remove toe tack.

- - - { ATTACH FOOTBED BEFORE FELTING } - - -

[1] Pin and sew Footbed in place, leaving heel open.

- - - - - { SHAPING AFTER FELTING } - - - -

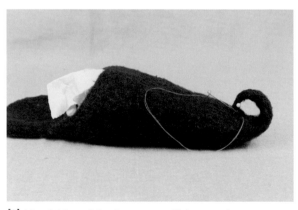

[2] After felting, while slippers are still damp, tack toes in curled shape and stuff with newsprint to shape.

Soling

These Slippers work best with a full suede sole. Follow directions on page 20 to make a template, cut sole out of suede, and then apply to the bottom of Slippers. When tracing template, follow outline of Slipper sole about 1" (2.5 cm) up curled toe so suede sole will extend to that point [1].

Lining

To make a lining template, trim template you made for sole so that toe is rounded and follows shape of Footbed. Using lining template, trace and then cut out two cardboard lining pieces. Insert cardboard lining into Slipper footbed [2]. Sew heel seam to secure cardboard in place [3].

[1] Make template for soling, following outline of Slipper sole about 1" (2.5 cm) up curled toe so the suede sole will extend to that point.

[2] Insert cardboard liner.

[3] Sew back seam to secure cardboard liner in place.

Needle Felting

Fold bubble wrap in half and roll it to fit inside Slipper. Trace felting template onto paper; cut out and lay in position on Slipper. Trace around template with tailor's chalk. Using a thin "rope" of roving that you have lightly twisted, cover chalk line with roving and, using felting needle, needle felt roving along outline. Using template as a reference, add remaining needle-felted details [1].

Beading

Refer to needle felting and beading template for sequin and seed bead placement.

Sequin and Seed Bead: Thread embroidery needle with 1 strand of thread or embroidery floss to match sequins, and knot floss. Bring needle from WS of Slipper up through sequin, through 1 bead, back down through sequin, then through to WS of Slipper [2]. Continue adding sequins and seed beads in this manner. Secure thread on WS after final sequin.

Seed Bead Alone: Thread embroidery needle with 1 strand of thread or embroidery floss to match beads, and knot floss. Bring needle up from WS of Slipper, through seed bead (sliding bead down to Slipper), then back through Slipper to WS in the same location. Continue adding seed beads in this manner. Secure thread on WS after final seed bead.

[1] After tracing around template with tailor's chalk, needle felt around roving and then fill in details.

[2] To apply sequins and beads together, bring needle up through sequin, then through bead, then down in through sequin to inside of Slipper. Continue using the same thread until you reach final sequin, then secure thread on inside of Slipper.

{ NEEDLE-FELTING AND BEADING TEMPLATE }

= sequin with seed bead stacked on top

• = seed bead alone

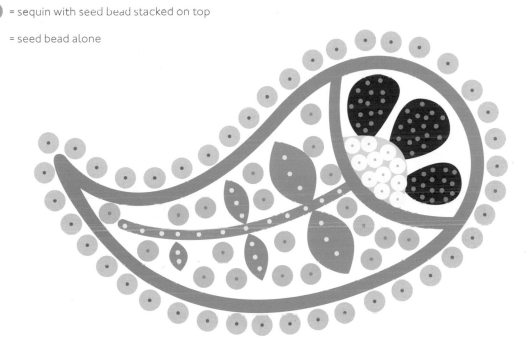

Another nod to my childhood fascination with moccasins, these ankle boots are stylish and cozy. I added a thick leather sole so that I would be able to wear them outside.

SIZES
Women's Small (Medium, Large)

FINISHED MEASUREMENTS
12 (13¼, 14½)" [30.5 (33.5, 37) cm] Foot length, before felting
9 (10, 11)" [23 (25.5, 28) cm] Foot length, after felting

YARN
Manos del Uruguay Wool Clasica [100% wool; 138 yards (125 meters) / 100 grams]: 2 hanks #X Topaz

NEEDLES
One set of five double-pointed needles (dpn) size US 10½ (6.5 mm); change needle size if necessary to obtain correct gauge

NOTIONS
Crochet hook size US J/10 (5.5 mm), or smaller (optional); stitch markers; tapestry needle; newsprint; disposable razor; one 12 x 12" (30.5 x 30.5 cm) piece of 6-ounce (171-gram) vegetable-tanned leather; leather hole punch; utility knife or leather shears; twenty ½" (1.5 cm) long bone beads; approximately 100 turquoise size 6 rocaille beads; elastic thread; embroidery floss; sewing needle; sewing thread; sewing machine; ⅛ yard wool fabric or large wool sweater, unfelted, for lining

GAUGE
12 sts and 16 rows = 4" (10 cm) in Stockinette stitch (St st), before felting

OVERVIEW
The Body of the Boots is worked in the round from the cuff down, shaping the Foot as you go. The Sole is worked from the Body stitches, then the bound-off edge is folded in half and sewn together. The Fringe is worked just below the top of the cuff, then the Boots are felted.

BODY
CO 36 (38, 40) sts. Join for working in the rnd, being careful not to twist sts; pm for beginning of the rnd. Begin St st (knit every rnd); work even for 2 (3, 3) rnds.

Shape Body
Increase Rnd 1: K11 (12, 12), k1-f/b, k11 (11, 13), k1-f/b, knit to last st, k1-f/b—39 (41, 43) sts. Knit 1 rnd.
Increase Rnd 2: K12 (13, 13), k1-f/b, k12 (12, 14), k1-f/b, knit to last st, k1-f/b—42 (44, 46) sts. Knit 4 (4, 4) rnds.

Increase Rnd 3: K19 (20, 21), k1-f/b, pm, k2, k1-f/b, knit to end—44 (46, 48) sts. Knit 2 rnds.
Increase Rnd 4: Knit to 1 st before marker, k1-f/b, sm, k2, k1-f/b, knit to end—46 (48, 50) sts. Knit 2 rnds.
Repeat Increase Rnd 4 once—48 (50, 52) sts. Knit 2 rnds.
Increase Rnd 5: Knit to 2 sts before marker, k1-f/b, k1, sm, k3, k1-f/b, knit to end—50 (52, 54) sts.
Repeat Increase Row 5 fourteen (17, 20) times—78 (86, 94) sts. Knit 3 (4, 5) rnds.

SOLE

Decrease Row 1: Change to working back and forth. K1, k2tog, k32 (36, 40), [k2tog, k1] twice, k2tog, k32 (36, 40), k2tog, k1 —73 (81, 89) sts remain. Knit 1 row.

Decrease Row 2: K1, k2tog, k29 (33, 37), [k2tog, k1] twice, k2tog, k30 (34, 38), k2tog, k1 —68 (76, 84) sts remain. Knit 1 row.

Decrease Row 3: K1, k2tog, k27 (31, 35), [k2tog, k1] twice, k2tog, k27 (31, 35), k2tog, k1 —63 (71, 79) sts remain. Knit 1 row.

Decrease Row 4: K1, k2tog, k25 (29, 33), [k2tog, k1] twice, k2tog, k24 (28, 32), k2tog, k1 —58 (66, 74) sts remain. Knit 0 (1, 1) row(s).

Decrease Row 5: K1, k2tog, k22 (26, 30), [k2tog, k1] twice, k2tog, k22 (26, 30), k2tog, k1 —53 (61, 69) sts remain. Knit 0 (1, 1) row(s).

Decrease Row 6: K1, k2tog, k19 (23, 27), [k2tog, k1], k2tog, k20 (24, 28), k2tog, k1 —48 (56, 64) sts remain. Knit 0 (1, 1) row(s).

Decrease Row 7: K1, k2tog, k17 (21, 25), [k2tog] 4 times, k17 (21, 25), k2tog, k1 —42 (50, 58) sts remain. BO all sts.

FINISHING

Fold Boot in half lengthwise, with fold line at heel and toe. Sew BO edge together from heel to toe.

Fringe

Cut approximately 18 (19, 20) lengths of yarn 7" (18 cm) long. Fold strand in half and insert looped end through tapestry needle. With RS of Body facing, working 4 rows down from CO edge, insert needle from bottom to top under bar between 2 sts [1], pull loop through bar, remove loop from needle, insert ends of yarn through loop, and pull to tighten [2]. Skip 1 st and work another Fringe [3]. Continue around. Trim ends evenly [4].

[1] Insert needle from bottom to top under bar between 2 sts.

[2] Insert ends of yarn through loop and pull to tighten.

[3] Skip 1 st and work another Fringe.

[4] Continue in this manner until you are back at first fringe. Trim ends evenly.

Felting

Felt Boots (see page 14). *Note: These Boots felt well in washing machine. When you stop machine to check progress, pull apart Fringes so they do not felt together. Do not turn Boots inside out, as Fringes will felt together.* While piece is still damp, stuff with newsprint to shape. Round toe into a pleasing shape and tug Sole to finished length. Pull Fringe into place and smooth down [5]. Trim ends evenly. To remove excess fuzz, shave piece with disposable razor. Allow to dry thoroughly.

Soling and Lining

Add soling (see page 18) and lining (see page 22) of your choice. I chose a sewn wool lining and leather soling for my slippers.

Beading

**Using sewing needle and 2 strands of elastic thread held together, or 1 strand of embroidery floss, knot thread on WS of Slipper, about ¼" (.5 cm) below top edge. Bring needle through to RS and *thread 3 rocaille beads, one bone bead, then 3 more rocaille beads onto needle [6]. Bring needle to WS, then back out to RS at starting point, making sure the beads are secure and lie flat but are not too tight.

Bring needle back through same beads again, then to WS.* Bring needle to RS, ⅜" (1 cm) from last bead; repeat from * to * once [7]. Secure thread on WS and cut. Repeat from ** until you have worked beads around entire Cuff. If you use embroidery floss rather than elastic thread, do not use a continuous length of thread for more than one bead unit (3 rocaille beads, one bone bead, and 3 rocaille beads); if you do, top of slipper will be too tight to fit over leg comfortably.

[5] After felting, while Boots are still damp, stuff with newsprint to shape and pull Fringe into place and smooth down.

- - - - - - { BEADING } - - - - - - -

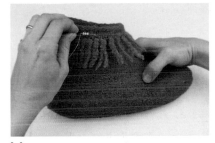

[6] Bring needle from back to front and thread on 3 rocaille beads, one bone bead, and 3 more rocaille beads.

[7] Work each unit of 7 beads on its own. Do not use a continuous length of thread.

The contrasting knitted uppers and felted sole give these adorable booties a dash of modern style. To create the roll-top upper, stitches are picked up from eyelets in the felted sole and knitted.

SIZES
0-6 (6-12, 12-18) months

FINISHED MEASUREMENTS
4 (4½, 5)" [10 (11.5, 12.5) cm] Foot length, after felting Sole

YARN
Brown Sheep Lamb's Pride Worsted [85% wool / 15% mohair; 190 yards (173 meters) / 4 ounces (114 grams)]: 1 skein #M187 Turquoise Depths (A)

Cascade Yarns Cascade 220 Heathers [100% Peruvian Highland wool; 220 yards (200 meters) / 100 grams): 1 hank #8012 Doeskin Heather (B)

NEEDLES
One set of five double-pointed needles (dpn) size US 10½ (6.5 mm); one set of five double pointed needles size US 4 (3.5 mm); change needle size if necessary to obtain correct gauge

NOTIONS
Crochet hook size US 4 (3.5 mm) or one size smaller or larger; stitch marker; non-felting waste yarn

GAUGE
14 sts and 18 rows = 4" (10 cm) in Stockinette stitch (St st), using larger needles and A, before felting
24 sts and 32 rows = 4" (10 cm) in St st, using smaller needles and B

OVERVIEW

The Sole is worked back and forth, with increases for the toe and heel, and a final eyelet row is worked before binding off. The cast-on and shaped side edges are sewn together and the Sole is felted. Then stitches are picked up for the Upper through the eyelet row in the felted Sole, and the Upper is worked in the round, with simple shaping.

SOLE

Using larger needles and A, CO 20 (24, 24) sts. Place marker after st 10 (12, 12).

Shape Sole

Increase Row 1 (RS): K 1, k 1-f/b, knit to 1 st before marker, k 1-f/b, sm, k 1-f/b, knit to last 2 sts, k 1-f/b, k 1—24 (28, 28) sts. Purl 1 row.
Repeat Increase Row 1 once—28 (32, 32) sts.
Increase Row 2 (WS): P 1, p 1-f/b, purl to 1 st before marker, p 1-f/b, sm, p 1-f/b, purl to last 2 sts, p 1-f/b, p 1—32 (36, 36) sts.
Repeat Increase Row 1 once, then Increase Row 2 once—40 (44, 44) sts.

SIZES SMALL AND MEDIUM ONLY

Knit 3 rows. Purl 1 row.

SIZE LARGE ONLY

Increase Row 3 (RS): K 1, k 1-f/b, knit to 1 st before marker, k 1-f/b, sm, k 1-f/b, knit to last 2 sts, k 1-f/b, k 1—48 sts.
Purl 3 rows. Knit 1 row. Purl 1 row.

ALL SIZES

Eyelet Row (RS): K 1, *yo, k2tog; repeat from * to last st, yo, k 1. BO all sts purlwise. Tie piece of non-felting string in center back eyelet.

FINISHING

Fold Sole in half widthwise. Sew CO and side edges together.

Felt well by hand (see page 14). Don't worry if the eyelets felt partially closed; just be sure you can still feel where they are. The finished Slipper looks better if the eyelets are small. You may open them a bit with a knitting needle if they are disappearing, but otherwise, let them felt up a bit.

Soling

Add soling of your choice (see page 18). Sample shown with paint-on latex.

UPPER

Remove non-felting string from center back eyelet. Using crochet hook and B, pick up st by pulling yarn through center back eyelet and placing it on smaller needle [1]. Continue to pick up 1 st through each eyelet around Sole, working in a clockwise direction [2] —20 (22, 24) sts. Distribute sts among 3 needles. Join for working in the rnd; pm for beginning of rnd.

Rnd 1: *K 1, using Backward Loop CO (see Special Techniques, page 151), CO 2 sts; repeat from * to end—60 (66, 72) sts.

Rnds 2-4, 6, 8, 10, 12, 14, and 16: Knit.

Rnd 5: K9 (12, 15), k2tog, [k5, k2tog] 5 times, k 14 (17, 20)—54 (60, 66) sts remain.

Rnd 7: K9 (12, 15), k2tog, [k4, k2tog] 5 times, k 13 (16, 19)—48 (54, 60) sts remain.

Rnd 9: K9 (12, 15), k2tog, [k3, k2tog] 5 times, k 12 (15, 18)—42 (48, 54) sts remain.

Rnd 11: K9 (12, 15), k2tog, [k2, k2tog] 5 times, k 11 (14, 17)—36 (42, 48) sts remain.

Rnd 13: K9 (12, 15), k2tog, [k 1, k2tog] 5 times, k 10 (13, 16)—30 (36, 42) sts remain.

Rnd 15: K9 (12, 15), [k2tog] 6 times, k9 (12, 15)—24 (30, 36) sts remain.

Knit 8 (8, 10) rounds. BO all sts loosely.

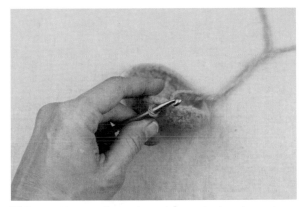

[1] To start Upper, pull yarn through center back eyelet.

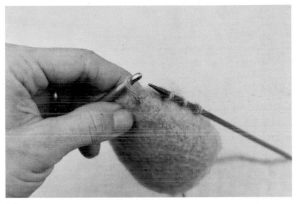

[2] Continue picking up 1 st through each eyelet around Sole clockwise.

Lightweight and easy to pack, these slippers bring the comforts of home to any location. They have lots of stretch, so they also make a great gift even if you don't know the lucky recipient's foot size.

SIZES

Women's Small (Medium, Large)

FINISHED MEASUREMENTS

7¾ (8½, 9¼)" [19.5 (21.5, 23.5) cm] Foot length
Note: Slippers should be worn with negative ease.

YARN

Madelinetosh Tosh Sock [100% superwash wool; 395 yards (361 meters) / 100 grams]: 1 hank Isadora

NEEDLES

One pair straight needles size US 3 (3.25 mm); one set of five double-pointed needles (dpn) size US 3 (3.25 mm); change needle size if necessary to obtain correct gauge

NOTIONS

Crochet hook size US D/3 (3.25 mm) or one size larger; stitch markers; waste yarn

GAUGE

28 sts and 50 rows = 4" (10 cm) in Garter stitch (knit every row)

OVERVIEW

The Foot is worked back and forth to the Toe, then sts are cast on on either side of the Foot and the Toe is shaped. The Toe and Heel seams are sewn, then an Attached I-Cord Foot Edging is worked around the Foot opening.

FOOT

CO 34 (36, 38) sts. Begin Garter st (knit every row); work even until piece measures 5½ (6¼, 7)" [14 (16, 18) cm] from beginning.

TOE

Next Row (RS): Continuing in Garter st and using Backward Loop CO (see Special Techniques, page 152), CO 3 (4, 5) sts at beginning of next 2 rows—40 (44, 48) sts. Knit 12 rows. Place marker 10 (11, 12) sts in from each edge.

Shape Toe

Decrease Row (RS): [Knit to 3 sts before marker, k2tog, k1, sm, k1, k2tog] twice, knit to end—36 (40, 44) sts remain. Knit 1 row. Repeat Decrease Row every other row 6 (7, 8) times—12 sts remain. Cut yarn, leaving a 6" (15 cm) tail; thread through remaining sts, pull tight, and fasten off.

FINISHING

Sew heel and toe seams.

Foot Edging

Using dpns and beginning at heel seam, pick up and knit 34 (38, 42) sts from purl bumps along top edge of Foot, 10 (12, 14) sts across Toe, then 34 (38, 42) sts from purl bumps along remaining top edge of Foot—78 (88, 98) sts. Cut yarn; do not join. Divide sts among 3 dpns. Using crochet hook, waste yarn, and Provisional CO (see Special Techniques, page 152), CO 4 sts onto empty dpn. Change to working yarn. Work Attached I-Cord as follows: K3, k2tog-tbl (last st from I-Cord together with 1 picked-up st), *slide sts back to right-hand end of dpn; using empty dpn, working sts from right to left, and pulling yarn from left to right for first st, k3, k2tog-tbl (last st from I-Cord together with 1 picked-up st); repeat from * around entire Foot edge until 4 sts remain, working even rows between pick-up rows if necessary so that I-Cord is smooth. Join ends using Kitchener st (see Special Techniques, page 151).

These thick, felted boots were inspired by the colorful pull-on rain boots my sons and nephews wear. While these won't work for puddle-jumping, they will keep little feet toasty and dry indoors.

SIZES
Child's X-Small (Small, Medium, Large)

FINISHED MEASUREMENTS
9 1/4 (10 1/4, 11 1/2, 11 1/2)" [23.5 (26, 29, 29) cm] Foot circumference, before felting
6 (6 1/2, 6 1/2, 7 1/2, 7 1/2)" [15 (16.5, 16.5, 19, 19) cm] Foot circumference, after felting
8 1/4 (9 1/2, 10 3/4, 12 1/4)" [21 (24, 27, 31) cm] Foot length, before felting
6 (7, 8, 9)" [15 (18, 20.5, 23) cm] Foot length, after felting

YARN
Manos del Uruguay Wool Classica [100% wool; 138 yards (126 meters) / 100 grams]: 1 (1, 1, 2) skein(s) Lapis

NEEDLES
One set of five double-pointed needles (dpn) size US 10 1/2 (6.5 mm); change needle size if necessary to obtain correct gauge

NOTIONS
Stitch marker; sewing needle and thread to match yarn

GAUGE
14 sts and 16 rows = 4" (10 cm) in Stockinette stitch (St st), before felting

OVERVIEW

The Legs are worked in the round, with short-row Heel shaping. The Foot and shaped Toe are worked in the round. I-Cord Pull Loops are worked; the Boots and Loops are felted separately, then assembled.

LEG

CO 28 (32, 36, 36) sts. Join for working in the rnd, being careful not to twist sts; pm for beginning of rnd. Knit 2 rnds.

Next Rnd: *K6 (7, 8, 8), k1-f/b; repeat from * to end—32 (36, 40, 40) sts.

Eyelet Rnd: K4 (5, 6, 6), yo, k2tog, k4, yo, k2tog, k8 (10, 12, 12), yo, k2tog, k4, yo, k2tog, k4 (5, 6, 6). Knit 17 (19, 21, 23) rnds.

HEEL

Note: Heel is shaped using short rows (see Special Techniques, page 152); work wraps together with wrapped sts as you come to them.

Short Row 1 (RS): K8 (9, 10, 10), wrp-t.
Short Row 2 (WS): P16 (18, 20, 20), wrp-t.
Short Row 3: K15 (17, 19, 19), wrp-t.
Short Row 4: P14 (16, 18, 18), wrp-t.
Short Row 5: K13 (15, 17, 17), wrp-t.
Short Row 6: P12 (14, 16, 16), wrp-t.
Short Row 7: K11 (13, 15, 15), wrp-t.

Short Row 8: P10 (12, 14, 14), wrp-t.
Short Row 9: K9 (11, 13, 13), wrp-t.
Short Row 10: P8 (10, 12, 12), wrp-t.
Short Row 11: K9 (11, 13, 13), wrp-t.
Short Row 12: P10 (12, 14, 14), wrp-t.
Short Row 13: K11 (13, 15, 15), wrp-t.
Short Row 14: P12 (14, 16, 16), wrp-t.
Short Row 15: K13 (15, 17, 17) wrp-t.
Short Row 16: P14 (16, 18, 18) wrp-t.
Short Row 17: K15 (17, 19, 19) wrp-t.
Short Row 18: P16 (18, 20, 20) wrp-t.
Short Row 19: K8 (9, 10, 10), pm for beginning of rnd.

FOOT

Knit 18 (22, 26, 32) rnds.

TOE

SIZES MEDIUM AND LARGE ONLY

Decrease Rnd: [K7, ssk, k2, k2tog, k7] twice—36 sts remain.

SIZES SMALL, MEDIUM, AND LARGE ONLY
Decrease Rnd: [K6, ssk, k2, k2tog, k6] twice—32 sts remain.

ALL SIZES
Decrease Rnd 1: [K5, ssk, k2, k2tog, k5] twice—28 sts remain.
Decrease Rnd 2: [K4, ssk, k2, k2tog, k4] twice—24 sts remain.
Decrease Rnd 3: [K3, ssk, k2, k2tog, k3] twice—20 sts remain.
Decrease Rnd 4: [K2, ssk, k2, k2tog, k2] twice—16 sts remain.
Decrease Rnd 5: [K1, ssk, k2, k2tog, k1] twice—12 sts remain.
Decrease Rnd 6: *K2tog, repeat from * to end—6 sts remain. Cut yarn, leaving an 8" (20.5 cm) tail. Thread tail through remaining sts, pull tight, and fasten off.

PULL LOOPS (Make 4)
CO 3 sts. Work I-Cord 11" (28 cm) long (see Special Techniques, page 151).

FINISHING
Felting
Fell Boots and Pull Loops well by hand (see page 14). While Boots are still damp, stuff with newsprint to shape. Round toe into a pleasing shape and tug Sole to finished length. Stretch Pull Loops slightly before they dry to lengthen and straighten them. Allow to dry thoroughly. Tie knot in one end of Pull Loop; with knot on outside of Boot, slip opposite end of Pull Loop through one eyelet on Boot, then through second eyelet on same side and tie knot in end. Tack each knot to Boot so the loops stand up.

Soling
Add soling (see page 18) of your choice. I used paint-on latex for mine.

Because these clogs can accommodate a range of adult sizes, they are nice to have on hand for guests to slip on while visiting. The cotton-blend yarn is good for all-season wear; the jute sole adds body and structure.

SIZES
Women's Small (Women's Medium/Men's Small, Women's Large/Men's Medium, Men's Large)

FINISHED MEASUREMENTS
8½ (9½, 10½, 11½)" [21.5 (24, 26.5, 29) cm] Foot length. *Note: Clog is intended to be worn with approximately ½" (1.5 cm) negative ease.*

YARN
Spud & Chloë Outer [65% superwash wool / 35% organic cotton; 60 yards (55 meters) / 100 grams]: 1 (1, 1, 2) hank (s) #7205 Sequoia (MC)
SecureLine 3-ply jute twine [100% jute; 63 yards (60 meters)]: 1 ball (A)

NEEDLES
One pair straight needles size US 10½ (6.5 mm); one pair straight needles size US 13 (9 mm); change needle size if necessary to obtain correct gauge

NOTIONS
Stitch holder

GAUGE
12 sts and 16 rows = 4" (10 cm) in Stockinette stitch (St st), using smaller needles and 1 strand of MC
10 sts and 16 rows = 4" (10 cm) in Garter stitch (knit every row), using larger needles and 2 strands of A held together

OVERVIEW

The Sole is worked back and forth from side to side. The Upper is worked back and forth as well, with simple side shaping. Then the Upper is sewn to the Sole.

SOLE

Using smaller needles and 2 strands of A held together, CO 3 (4, 4, 5) sts. Knit 1 row.

Shape Sole
SIZES WOMEN'S SMALL AND MEN'S LARGE ONLY
Increase Row 1: K1 (-, -, 2), k1-f/b, k1 (-, -, 2)—4 (-, -, 6) sts. Knit 1 row.

ALL SIZES
Increase Row 2: K2 (2, 2, 3), M1, k2 (2, 2, 3)— 5 (5, 5, 7) sts. Knit 1 row.
Increase Row 3: K2 (2, 2, 3), k1-f/b, k2 (2, 2, 3)—6 (6, 6, 8) sts. Knit 1 row.
Increase Row 4: K3 (3, 3, 4), M1, k3 (3, 3, 4)—7 (7, 7, 9) sts. Knit 4 (6, 8, 10) rows.
Increase Row 5: K3 (3, 3, 4), k1-f/b, k3 (3, 3, 4)—8 (8, 8, 10) sts. Knit 15 (17, 18, 17) rows.
Decrease Row 1: K3 (3, 3, 4), skp, k3 (3, 3, 4)—7 (7, 7, 9) sts remain. Knit 4 (5, 6, 7) rows.
Decrease Row 2: Skp, k3 (3, 3, 5), skp—5 (5, 5, 7) sts remain. Knit 1 row.
Decrease Row 3: Skp, k1 (1, 1, 3), skp—3 (3, 3, 5) sts remain. BO all sts.

UPPER

Using smaller needles and 1 strand of MC, CO 8 (9, 10, 11) sts. Begin St st; purl 1 row.

Shape Upper
Note: Upper is shaped with a combination of increases and short rows (see Special Techniques, page 152); work wraps together with wrapped sts as you come to them.
Rows 1, 3, and 5: Purl.
Rows 2 and 4 (RS): K1, M1, knit to last st, M1, k1—12 (13, 14, 15) sts after Row 4.
Short Row 6: K11 (12, 13, 14) wrp-t.
Short Row 7: P10 (11, 12, 13) wrp-t.
Row 8: Knit.
Row 9: Purl.
Rows 10 and 11: Repeat Rows 2 and 3—14 (15, 16, 17) sts after Row 10.

Short Row 12: K13 (14, 15, 16) wrp-t.
Short Row 13: P12 (13, 14, 15) wrp-t.
Rows 14-17: Repeat Rows 8-11 — 16 (17, 18, 19) sts after Row 16.
Knit 12 (14, 16, 20) rows.
Next Row (RS): K6 and transfer to st holder, BO next 4 (5, 6, 7) sts, knit to end—6 sts remain.

Left Side

Working on 6 Left Side sts only, work even for 1 (1, 1, 3) row(s).
Decrease Row 1 (RS): K1, k2tog, k3 -5 sts remain. Purl 1 row.
Decrease Row 2 (RS): K1, k2tog, k2—4 sts remain. Purl 1 row.
Decrease Row 3 (RS): K1, k2tog, k1—3 sts remain. Work even for 1 (3, 3, 3) row(s).
Decrease Row 4 (RS): K1, k2tog—2 sts remain. BO all sts. Cut yarn.

Right Side

With WS facing, rejoin yarn to sts on holder. Work even for 1 (1, 1, 3) row(s).
Decrease Row 1 (RS): K3, skp, k1—5 sts remain. Purl 1 row.
Decrease Row 2 (RS): K2, skp, k1—4 sts remain. Purl 1 row.
Decrease Row 3 (RS): K1, skp, k1—3 sts remain. Work even for 1 (3, 3, 3) row(s).
Decrease Row 4 (RS): K1, skp—2 sts remain. BO all sts.

FINISHING

Sew Upper to Sole.

I call these loafers, but when I was designing them I was thinking about a cross between leather boat shoes and canvas espadrilles. The firm and sturdy jute sole makes them an ideal summertime house shoe for women and men.

SIZES
Women's Small (Women's Medium/Men's Small, Women's Large/Men's Medium, Men's Large)

FINISHED MEASUREMENTS
9 1/4 (10 1/4, 11 1/4, 12 1/2)" [23.5 (26, 29, 32) cm] Foot length
Note: Loafers are intended to be worn with approximately 1/2" (1.5 cm) negative ease.

YARN
Blue Sky Alpacas Worsted Cotton [100% organic cotton; 150 yards (137 meters) / 100 grams]: 1 (1, 1, 2) hank(s) #636 Jasper (MC)
SecureLine 3-ply jute twine [100% jute; 63 yards (60 meters)]: 1 ball (A)

NEEDLES
One pair double-pointed needles (dpn) size US 10 1/2 (6.5 mm); one set of five double-pointed needles size US 7 (4.5 mm); change needle size if necessary to obtain correct gauge

NOTIONS
Crochet hook size US K/10 1/2 (6.5 mm), or one size larger; stitch marker; safety pins; 24" (61 cm) 1/2" (1.5 cm) wide elastic; 1 yard (1 meter) leather lacing

GAUGE
14 sts and 28 rows = 4" (10 cm) in Garter st (knit every row), using larger needles and A
16 sts and 26 rows = 4" (10 cm) in Stockinette st (St st), using smaller needles and MC

OVERVIEW

A firm jute Sole is knit sideways first with short-row shaping. Then stitches are picked up to work the Upper, and a separate tongue is worked back and forth, then sewn on.

SOLE

Using crochet hook, waste yarn, and Provisional CO (see Special Techniques, page 152), CO 28 (32, 36, 40) sts. Change to larger needles and A. Knit 2 (2, 3, 3) rows.
Rows 1 and 2: K 1, M 1, knit to end—30 (34, 38, 42) sts after Row 2.
Row 3: Knit to last st, M 1, k 1 —31 (35, 39, 43) sts.

Shape Sole

Note: Sole is shaped using short rows (see Special Techniques, page 152); it is not necessary to work wraps together with wrapped sts.
Short Row 1: K 1, M 1, k 12, wrp-t—32 (36, 40, 44) sts.
Short Row 2: Knit to end.
Row 3: Knit.
Short Row 4: K 12, wrp-t.
Short Row 5: Knit to end.
Row 6: Knit.
Short Row 7: K 16, wrp-t.
Short Row 8: Knit to end.
Row 9: Knit.
Short Row 10: K 12, wrp-t.
Short Row 11: Knit to end.
Row 12: Knit.
Short Row 13: K 13, wrp-t.
Short Row 14: Knit to last 3 sts, skp, k 1 —31 (35, 39, 43) sts remain.

Row 15: K 1, skp, knit to end—30 (34, 38, 42) sts.
Rows 16 and 17: K 1, skp, knit to end—28 (32, 36, 40) sts remain after Row 17. Knit 2 (2, 3, 3) rows. Cut yarn; leave sts on needle. Carefully unravel Provisional CO and place live sts on smaller needle.

UPPER

With RS of Sole facing, using smaller needles and MC, and beginning at center of narrower side edge of Sole (heel), pick up and knit 4 sts, knit across 28 (32, 36, 40) Sole sts, pick up and knit 10 (10, 12, 12) sts across wider side edge (toe), knit across 28 (32, 36, 40) from Provisional CO, then pick up and knit 4 sts to center of right side edge—74 (82, 92, 100) sts. Join for working in the rnd; pm for beginning of rnd. Knit 7 (8, 9, 10) rnds.

Shape Casing
Next Row (RS): K27 (29, 32, 34), BO next 20 (24, 28, 32) sts, knit to end, removing marker—54 (58, 64, 68) sts. Cut yarn.
Next Row (RS): With RS facing, rejoin yarn to right-hand end of casing. Begin St st; work even for 3 rows. Knit 1 row (turning row). Work in St st for 3 rows. BO all sts purlwise.

TONGUE

Using smaller needles and MC, CO 13 (15, 17, 19) sts.
Purl 1 row.

Shape Tongue

Next Row (RS): K1, M1, knit to last st, M1, k1—15 (17, 19, 21) sts. Continuing in St st, work even for 14 (16, 18, 20) rows.

Decrease Row 1 (WS): P2tog, purl to last 2 sts, p2tog—13 (15, 17, 19) sts remain.

Decrease Row 2: Skp, knit to last 2 sts, k2tog—11 (13, 15, 17) sts remain.

Repeat Decrease Rows 1 and 2 one (1, 2, 2) time(s), then repeat Decrease Row 1 zero (1, 0, 1) time(s)—7 sts remain. BO all sts.

FINISHING

Fold casing to WS at Turning Row and sew to WS, being careful not to let sts show on RS; do not close ends of casing. Pin center of BO edge of Tongue to center of toe of Upper. Pin each side of Tongue just below casing, approximately 1" (2.5 cm) from CO edge of Tongue. Sew Tongue to Upper, between side pins, easing Tongue and Upper as necessary and leaving 1" (2.5 cm) Tongue flap.

Cut two pieces of elastic 4" (10 cm) shorter than casing length. Cut leather lacing in 4 equal pieces. Sew one piece of lacing to each end of each elastic. Pin one end of lacing to safety pin, and thread pin through casing. Tie lacing.

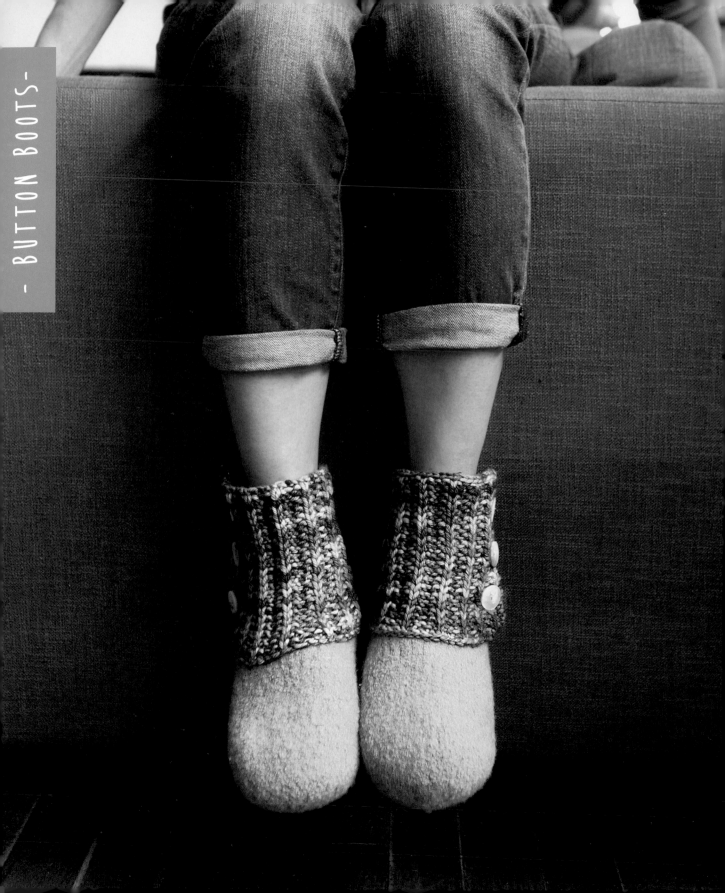

Children and adults will appreciate these thick and cushy slippers topped by a generous cuff that is reminiscent of old-fashioned spats. Button all the way up or fasten one button and fold down the cuff; the Cartridge Belt Rib is reversible, so it looks good both ways.

SIZES
Child's X-Small (Child's Small, Child's Medium, Child's Large/Women's Small, Women's Medium/Men's Small, Women's Large/Men's Medium, Men's Large)

FINISHED MEASUREMENTS
8¾ (9½, 10¼, 11¾, 13, 13¾, 14½)" [22 (24, 26, 30, 33, 35, 37) cm] Foot circumference, before felting
6 (6½, 7, 8, 9, 9½, 10)" [15 (16.5, 18, 20.5, 23, 24, 25.5) cm] Foot circumference, after felting
12½ (12¾, 13½, 14½, 15½, 16½, 17½)" [32 (32.5, 34.5, 37, 39.5, 42, 44.5) cm] Foot length, before felting
6 (7, 8, 9, 10, 11, 12)" [15 (18, 20.5, 23, 25.5, 28, 30.5) cm] Foot length, after felting

YARN
Malabrigo Merino Worsted [100% merino wool; 210 yards (192 meters) / 100 grams]: 1 (1, 1, 2, 2, 2, 3) hank(s) #505 Moss (A)

Malabrigo Rios [100% superwash merino wool; 210 yards (192 meters) / 100 grams]: 1 (1, 1, 1, 1, 2, 2) hank(s) #859 Primavera (B)

NEEDLES
One set of five double-pointed needles (dpn) size US 13 (9 mm); one set of five double-pointed needles size US 8 (5 mm); change needle size if necessary to obtain correct gauge

NOTIONS
Disposable razor; six 1" buttons; sewing needle and thread to match B

GAUGE
11 sts and 14 rows = 4" (10 cm) in Stockinette stitch (St st), using larger needles and 2 strands of A held together, before felting
20 sts and 36 rows = 4" in Cartridge Belt Rib, using smaller needles and 1 strand of B

OVERVIEW

The Sole is worked back and forth, then the Gusset is shaped using short rows. Stitches are picked up from the Gusset for the Foot and the Foot is worked for several rows, then stitches are cast on and the piece is joined and worked in the round to the Toe, which is shaped using short rows. The Cuff is worked in the second yarn, then set aside while the Boots are felted. Once felting is complete, the Cuff is sewn to the Boot.

STITCH PATTERN

Cartridge Belt Rib

(multiple of 4 sts + 3; 2-row repeat)

Row 1 (RS): K3, *slip 1 wyif, k3; repeat from * to end.

Row 2: K1, *slip 1 wyif, k3; repeat to last 2 sts, slip 1 wyif, k1.

Repeat Rows 1 and 2 for Cartridge Belt Rib.

HEEL FLAP

Using larger needles and 2 strands of A held together, CO 6 (6, 8, 8, 10, 10, 12) sts.

Row 1 (WS): Slip 1, purl to end.

Row 2: Slip 1, k1, M1, knit to last 2 sts, M1, k2—8 (8, 10, 10, 12, 12, 14) sts.

Row 3: Slip 1, purl to end.

Row 4: Slip 1, knit to end.

Repeat Rows 3 and 4 five (5, 6, 6, 7, 7, 8) times.

Shape Heel

Note: Gusset is shaped using short rows (see Special Techniques, page 152). Work wraps together with wrapped sts as you come to them.

Short Row 1 (WS): P5 (5, 7, 7, 9, 9, 11), p2tog, wrp-t—7 (7, 9, 9, 11, 11, 13) sts remain.

Short Row 2: K3 (3, 5, 5, 7, 7, 9), k2tog, wrp-t—6 (6, 8, 8, 10, 10, 12) sts remain.

Short Row 3: P3 (3, 5, 5, 7, 7, 9), wrp-t.

Short Row 4: K2 (2, 4, 4, 6, 6, 8), wrp-t.

Short Row 5: P1 (1, 3, 3, 5, 5, 7), wrp-t.

GUSSET

Row 1: K3 (3, 5, 5, 7, 7, 9), pick up and knit 6 (6, 7, 7, 8, 8, 9) sts from slipped sts along edge of Sole, turn—12 (12, 15, 15, 18, 18, 21) sts.

Row 2: Slip 1, purl to end, pick up and knit 6 (6, 7, 7, 8, 8, 9) sts from slipped sts along edge of Sole—18 (18, 22, 22, 26, 26, 30) sts.

Row 3: Slip 1, knit to end.

Row 4: Slip 1, purl to end.

Repeat Rows 3 and 4 seven times, then Row 3 once. Using Backward Loop CO (see Special Techniques, page 151), CO 1 (1, 1, 2, 2, 3, 2) st(s) at beginning of next 2 rows—20 (20, 24, 26, 30, 32, 34) sts. Purl 1 row.

FOOT

Next Row (RS): CO 4 (6, 4, 6, 6, 6, 6) sts, join for working in the rnd; pm for beginning of rnd, knit to end—24 (26, 28, 32, 36, 38, 40) sts. Knit 14 (15, 16, 19, 20, 23, 25) rnds.

TOE

Short Row 1 (RS): K1, wrp-t.

Short Row 2 (WS): P11 (12, 13, 14, 16, 17, 18) wrp-t.

Short Row 3: Knit to marker. Continuing to work in the rnd, knit 1 (1, 2, 2, 3, 3, 4) rnd(s).

Short Row 4: K1, wrp-t.

Short Row 5: P11 (12, 13, 14, 16, 17, 18), wrp-t.

Short Row 6: Knit to marker. Continuing to work in the rnd, knit 1 (1, 2, 2, 3, 3, 4) rnd(s).

SIZES CHILD'S SMALL AND WOMEN'S LARGE/MEN'S MEDIUM ONLY
Rnd 7: *K- (11, -, -, -, 17, -), k2tog; repeat from * to end—- (24, -, -, -, 36, -) sts remain.

ALL SIZES
Rnd 8: *K4 (4, 5, 6, 7, 7, 8), k2tog; repeat from * to end—20 (20, 24, 28, 32, 32, 36) sts remain.
Rnd 9: *K3 (3, 4, 5, 6, 6, 7), k2tog; repeat from * to end— 16 (16, 20, 24, 28, 28, 32) sts remain.
Rnd 10: *K2 (2, 3, 4, 5, 5, 6), k2tog; repeat from * to end— 12 (12, 16, 20, 24, 24, 28) sts remain.
Rnd 11: *K1 (1, 2, 3, 4, 4, 5), k2tog; repeat from * to end—8 (8, 12, 16, 20, 20, 24) sts remain.

SIZES CHILD'S MEDIUM, CHILD'S LARGE/WOMEN'S SMALL, WOMEN'S MEDIUM/MEN'S SMALL, WOMEN'S LARGE/MEN'S MEDIUM, AND MEN'S LARGE ONLY
Rnd 12: *K- (-, 1, 2, 3, 3, 4), k2tog; repeat from * to end—- (-, 8, 12, 16, 16, 20) sts remain.

SIZES CHILD'S LARGE/WOMEN'S SMALL, WOMEN'S MEDIUM/MEN'S SMALL, WOMEN'S LARGE/MEN'S MEDIUM, AND MEN'S LARGE ONLY
Rnd 13: *K- (-, -, 1, 2, 2, 3), k2tog; repeat from * to end—- (-, -, 8, 12, 12, 16) sts remain.

SIZES WOMEN'S MEDIUM/MEN'S SMALL, WOMEN'S LARGE/MEN'S MEDIUM, MEN'S LARGE ONLY
Rnd 14: *K- (-, -, -, 1, 1, 2), k2tog; repeat from * to end—- (-, -, -, 8, 8, 12) sts remain.

SIZE MEN'S LARGE ONLY
Rnd 15: *K1, k2tog; repeat from * to end—8 sts remain.

ALL SIZES
Cut yarn, leaving an 8" (20.5 cm) tail. Thread tail through remaining sts, pull tight, and fasten off.

CUFF
Using smaller needles and 1 strand of B, CO 39 (47, 51, 55, 67, 71, 75) sts. Begin Cartridge Belt Rib; work even for 7 (7, 7, 9, 9, 11, 11) rows
*Buttonhole Row (RS): K4, BO next 3 sts, work to end.
Next Row: Work to end, CO 3 sts over BO sts.
Work even for 8 (8, 10, 10, 12, 12) rows.
Repeat from * twice. BO all sts.

FINISHING
Felt Boots well (see page 14). While piece is still damp, stuff with newsprint to shape. Round toe into a pleasing shape and tug Sole to finished length. To remove excess fuzz, shave piece with a disposable razor. Allow to dry thoroughly. Sew buttons opposite buttonholes, ½" (1.5 cm) in from edge. Pin cuff to Foot, making sure to place buttons on outside of each Boot. Sew Cuff to Foot.

Soling
Add soling of your choice (see page 18). I used a paint-on latex for mine.

These loafer-style slippers are sturdy enough for trips to the mailbox but cozy enough for curling up on the couch.

SIZES
Child's Large/Women's Small (Women's Medium/Men's Small, Women's Large/Men's Medium, Men's Large)

FINISHED MEASUREMENTS
11 1/4 (11 1/4, 12 1/4, 12 1/4)" [28.5 (28.5, 31, 32.5) cm] Foot circumference, before felting
10 (10, 10 3/4, 11 1/4) [25.5 (25.5, 27, 28.5) cm] Foot circumference, after felting
Note. Slippers require a lining to fit well, as there is ease built into the circumference to accommodate the lining.
10 3/4 (12, 13 1/4, 14 1/2)" [27 (30.5, 33.5, 37) cm] Foot length, before felting
9 (10, 11, 12)" [23 (25.5, 28, 30.5) cm] Foot length, after felting

YARN
Brown Sheep Company Lamb's Pride Worsted (85% wool / 15% mohair; 190 yards [174 meters] / 4 ounces [114 grams]): 2 skeins #M186 Golden Mushroom (MC); 1 skein #M181 Prairie Fire (A)

NEEDLES
One set of five double-pointed needles (dpn) size US 13 (9 mm); one set of five double-pointed needles size US 10 1/2 (6.5 mm); change needle size if necessary to obtain correct gauge

NOTIONS
Stitch marker; newsprint; disposable razor; piece of shearling large enough to accommodate two linings; craft glue; piece of suede the same size as shearling; double-sided tape, leather needle, embroidery floss or heavy-duty thread to match yarn

GAUGE
10 sts and 16 rows = 4" (10 cm) in Stockinette stitch (St st), using larger needles and 2 strands of MC held together, before felting
16 sts and 16 rows = 4" (10 cm) in Fair Isle Pattern, using smaller needles before felting

OVERVIEW

The Upper is worked back and forth from the Fair Isle Chart, then the Toe is shaped. The Sides are picked up from the Upper and the Heel is shaped using short rows. Once the Heel has been shaped, the Sole is then worked until the stitches meet in the center of the Sole, where the sides are joined using 3-Needle Bind-Off.

UPPER

Using smaller needles and 1 strand of MC, CO 21 sts. Begin Fair Isle Pattern from Chart; work Rows 1-14 once, then Rows 1-7 (7, 12, 12) once.

Shape Toe

Next Row (RS): Continuing to work Fair Isle Pattern, BO 4 sts at beginning of row once, 5 sts once, then 1 st 3 times. BO remaining 9 sts.
Note: Uneven BOs will even out in the felting.

SIDES

Using larger needles, 2 strands of MC held together, and Backward Loop CO (see Special Techniques, page 151), CO 12 (14, 15, 18) sts; do not turn. With RS of Upper facing, beginning at CO edge, pick up and knit 24 (24, 28, 28) sts evenly spaced along right side edge, BO edge, and left side edge; CO 12 (14, 15, 18) sts—48 (52, 58, 64) sts. Join for working in the rnd; pm for beginning of rnd. Knit 1 rnd.

Shape Heel

Note: Heel is shaped using short-row shaping (see Special Techniques, page 152); work wraps together with wrapped sts as you come to them.
Short Row 1 (RS): K6 (6, 7, 8), wrp-t.
Short Row 2 (WS): P12 (12, 14, 16), wrp-t, knit to end.

SIZE CHILD'S LARGE/WOMEN'S SMALL ONLY

Next Rnd: *K7, k1-f/b; repeat from * to end—54 sts.

SIZE WOMEN'S MEDIUM/MEN'S SMALL ONLY

Next Rnd: *K6, k1-f/b, k5, k1-f/b; repeat from * to end—60 sts.

SIZE WOMEN'S LARGE/MEN'S MEDIUM ONLY

Next Rnd: *K6, k1-f/b, k7, k1-f/b, [k6, k1-f/b] twice; repeat from * to end—66 sts.

SIZE MEN'S LARGE ONLY

Next Rnd: *K7, k1-f/b; repeat from * to end—72 sts.

ALL SIZES

Short Row 3 (RS): K5 (5, 6, 7), wrp-t.
Short Row 4 (WS): P10 (10, 12, 14) wrp-t, knit to end. Knit 6 (6, 7, 7) rnds.

SOLE

Row 1 (RS): Change to working back and forth. Knit, removing marker.
Row 2 (WS): K1, k2tog, k20 (23, 26, 29), [k2tog, k1] twice, k2tog, knit to last 3 sts, k2tog, k1—49 (55, 61, 67) sts remain.
Row 3: Knit.
Row 4: K1, k2tog, k17 (20, 23, 26), [k2tog, k1] twice, k2tog, knit to last 3 sts, k2tog, k1—44 (50, 56, 62) sts remain.
Row 5: Knit.
Row 6: K1, k2tog, k15 (18, 21, 24), [k2tog, k1] twice, k2tog, knit to last 3 sts, k2tog, k1—39 (45, 51, 57) sts remain. Knit 0 (0, 1, 1) row(s).
Row 7 (7, 8, 8): K1, k2tog, k13 (16, 19, 22), [k2tog, k1] twice, k2tog, knit to last 3 sts, k2tog, k1—34 (40, 46, 52) sts remain. Divide Sole sts in half and BO all sts using 3-Needle BO (see Special Techniques, page 152). Sew short sides of Sole together.

--------------------- { FAIR ISLE CHART } ---------------------

Fair Isle Pattern

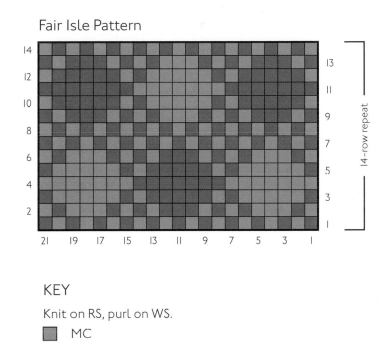

KEY

Knit on RS, purl on WS.

⬛ MC

⬛ A

FINISHING

Felt Sole and Upper to measurements (see page 14). While piece is still damp, stuff with newsprint to form Upper. Round toe into a pleasing shape and tug Sole to finished length. To remove excess fuzz and show off the Fair Isle Pattern, shave piece with disposable razor. Allow to dry thoroughly.

Soling and Lining

Add soling (see page 18) and lining (see page 22) of your choice. I chose a sewn-on suede sole and shearling lining for my Loafers.

These convertible slippers can be worn full length so that the knitted fabric covers both the feet and the lower legs, or they can be folded over (as shown) so the feet are exposed. Worked in the round with an elastic rib stitch, these simple booties will fit growing babies for a long time.

SIZES
1–3 (3–6, 6–12, 12–18) months

FINISHED MEASUREMENTS
5 1/4 (5 3/4, 6 1/4, 6 1/4)" [13.5 (14.5, 16, 16) cm] circumference
7 (8, 9 1/2, 11)" [18 (20.5, 24, 28) cm] Foot length

YARN
Malabrigo Yarn Arroyo [100% superwash merino wool; 335 yards (306 meters) / 100 grams]: 1 hank #49 Jupiter

NEEDLES
One set of five double-pointed needles (dpn) size US 3 (3.25 mm); change needle size if necessary to obtain correct gauge

NOTIONS
Stitch marker

GAUGE
28 sts and 36 rows = 4" (10 cm) in 2x2 Rib, slightly stretched

OVERVIEW
The Body is worked in the round to the Sole, which is worked back and forth, then bound off. The Sole is folded over the opening and sewn into place.

STITCH PATTERN
2x2 Rib
(multiple of 4 sts; 1-rnd repeat)
All Rnds: *K2, p2; repeat from * to end.

BODY
CO 36 (40, 44, 44) sts. Join for working in the rnd, being careful not to twist sts; pm for beginning of rnd. Begin 2x2 Rib; work even until piece measures 7 (8, 9 1/2, 11)" [18 (20.5, 24, 28) cm] from the beginning.

SOLE
BO 16 (18, 20, 20) sts—20 (22, 24, 24) sts remain.
Working back and forth in pattern as established, work even until piece measures 2 (2, 2 1/2, 3)" [5 (5, 6.5, 7.5) cm] from BO row, ending with a WS row. BO all sts in pattern.

FINISHING
Fold Sole to RS and sew side edges to Body of Legwarmer. Leave BO edge unseen.

SPECIAL TECHNIQUES

Backward Loop CO: Make a loop (using a slip knot) with the working yarn and place it on the right-hand needle (first st CO), *wind yarn around thumb clockwise, insert right-hand needle into the front of the loop on thumb, remove thumb and tighten st on needle; repeat from * for remaining sts to be CO, or for casting on at the end of a row in progress.

I-Cord: Using a double-pointed needle, cast on or pick up the required number of sts; the working yarn will be at the left-hand side of the needle. *Transfer the needle with the sts to your left hand, bring the yarn around behind the work to the right-hand side; using a second double-pointed needle, knit the sts from right to left, pulling the yarn from left to right for the first st; do not turn. Slide the sts to the opposite end of the needle; repeat from * until the I-Cord is the desired length. *Note: After a few rows, the tubular shape will become apparent.*

Kitchener Stitch: Using a blunt tapestry needle, thread a length of yarn approximately 4 times the length of the section to be joined. Hold the pieces to be joined WSs together, with the needles holding the sts parallel, both ends pointing to the right. Working from right to left, insert tapestry needle into first st on front needle as if to purl, and pull yarn through, leaving st on needle; insert tapestry needle into first st on back needle as if to knit, and pull yarn through, leaving st on needle; *insert tapestry needle into first st on front needle as if to knit, pull yarn through, and remove st from needle, insert tapestry needle into next st on front needle as if to purl, and pull yarn through, leaving st on needle; insert tapestry needle into first st on back needle as if

to purl, pull yarn through, and remove st from needle; insert tapestry needle into next st on back needle as if to knit, pull yarn through, leave st on needle. Repeat from *, working 3 or 4 sts at a time, then go back and adjust tension to match the pieces being joined. When 1 st remains on each needle, cut yarn and pass through last 2 sts to fasten off.

Needle Felting: Needle felting is different from wet felting, as you use a special barbed needle to felt fibers together. The projects in this book use the technique of applying wool roving to a felted wool background. To needle felt, you need a felting needle in any size (available at well-stocked yarn shops and craft stores) and a felting surface that will protect the work surface underneath and the fragile needles. Thick foam pads are often used, but you can also roll up bubble wrap and place it inside slippers if you are felting on the slipper toe or upper. Wool roving is most often used for needle-felted embellishments, though you can also untwist wool yarn and felt that into place, which is a nice way to make delicate lines or a small feature.

To transfer a design to your work surface, photocopy then cut out the template and place it into position on the item to be felted. Trace around it using chalk. Pull off a small piece of roving and lay it on the area to be covered. Jab needle in and out of the wool roving until it is secured to the base fabric. Be sure to hold the needle perpendicular to the work surface, not at an angle, as the needles are brittle and break easily. It's easiest to begin with a small amount of roving and then add more as you go, building up the shape in layers.

Provisional CO: Using a crochet hook and smooth yarn (crochet cotton or ravel cord used for machine knitting), work a crochet chain with a few more chains than the number of sts needed; fasten off. If desired, tie a knot on the fastened-off end to mark the end that you will be unraveling from later. Turn the chain over; with a needle one size smaller than required for the piece and working yarn, starting a few chains in from the beginning of the chain, pick up and knit 1 st in each bump at the back of the chain, leaving any extra chains at the end unworked. Change to needle size required for project on first row. When ready to work the live sts, unravel the chain by loosening the fastened-off end and "unzipping" the chain, placing the live sts on a spare needle.

Running Stitch: *Insert threaded needle from RS of fabric to WS and back to RS a few times, moving forward each time, then pull through to WS. Repeat from * for desired length of line.

Short-Row Shaping: Work the number of sts specified in the instructions, then wrap and turn (wrp-t) as follows: To wrap a knit st, bring yarn to the front (purl position), slip the next st purlwise to the right-hand needle, bring yarn to the back of work, return the slipped st on the right-hand needle to the left-hand needle purlwise; turn, ready to work the next row, leaving the remaining sts unworked. To wrap a purl st, work as for wrapping a knit st, but bring yarn to the back (knit position) before slipping the st, and to the front after slipping the st.

When short rows are completed, or when working progressively longer short rows, work the wrap together with the wrapped st as you come to it as follows: If st is to be worked as a knit st, insert the right-hand needle into the wrap from below, then into the wrapped st; k2tog; if st to be worked is a purl st, insert needle into the wrapped st, then down into the wrap; p2tog. (Wrap may be lifted onto the left-hand needle, then worked together with the wrapped st if this is easier.)

3-Needle BO: Place the sts to be joined onto two same-size needles; hold the pieces to be joined with RSs facing each other and the needles parallel, both pointing to the right. Holding both needles in your left hand, using working yarn and a third needle the same size or one size larger, insert third needle into first st on front needle, then into first st on back needle; knit these 2 sts together; *knit next st from each needle together (two sts on right-hand needle); pass first st over second st to BO 1 st. Repeat from * until 1 st remains on third needle; cut yarn and fasten off.

Right: Cotton Loafers (page 137).

ABBREVIATIONS

BO – Bind off
Circ – Circular
CO – Cast on
Dpn – Double-pointed needle(s)
K1-f/b – Knit into the front and back loop of the same stitch to increase 1 stitch.
K1-tbl – Knit 1 stitch through the back loop.
K2tog – Knit 2 stitches together.
K3tog – Knit 3 stitches together.
K – Knit
M1 (make 1) – With the tip of the left-hand needle inserted from front to back, lift the strand between the two needles onto the left-hand needle; knit the strand through the back loop to increase 1 stitch.
P1-f/b – Purl into the front and back loop of the same stitch to increase 1 stitch.
P2tog – Purl 2 stitches together.
P3tog – Purl 3 stitches together.
Pm – Place marker
P – Purl
Rnd(s) – Round(s)
RS – Right side
Skp (slip, knit, pass) – Slip the next stitch knitwise to the right-hand needle, k1, and pass the slipped stitch over the knit stitch.
Sm – Slip marker
Ssk (slip, slip, knit) – Slip the next 2 stitches to the right-hand needle one at a time as if to knit; return them to the left-hand needle one at a time in their new orientation; knit them together through the back loops.
St(s) – Stitch(es)
Tbl – Through the back loop
Tog – Together
WS – Wrong side
Wrp-t – Wrap and turn (see Special Techniques, Short-Row Shaping, page 152)
Wyif – With yarn in front
Yo – Yarnover

Left to right: Pull-On "Puddle" Boots (page 129), Fireside Booties (page 29), and Ankle Fringe Boots (page 119).

Resources

ONLINE SUPPORT

www.duofiberworks.com
This is my blog, where I share tutorials, videos, and patterns for many felted knits. In conjunction with this book, I have created videos on hand felting, fixing holes, shaping and shaving felted projects, lining, soling, making recycled and felted fringe, and embellishing with needle felting, beads, and sequins.

www.ravelry.com
I'm active on Ravelry and would love to connect with you there. My username is katiemfree and my designer name is Katie Startzman. Look me up, I can't wait to see your slipper projects! There's also a group for this book on Ravelry: www.ravelry .com/groups/the-knitted-slipper-book. Join us and chat about slipper knitting, find answers to frequently asked questions, or just share what you're working on.

SUPPLIES

If you can't find the supplies I've called for at your favorite local retailer, contact the manufacturers and distributors listed below.

Yarn
Blue Sky Alpacas
www.blueskyalpacas.com

Brooklyn Tweed
www.brooklyntweed.net

Brown Sheep Company, Inc.
www.brownsheep.com

Cascade Yarns
www.cascadeyarns.com

Knitting Fever
www.knittingfever.com

Madelinetosh
www.madelinetosh.com

Malabrigo
www.malabrigoyarn.com

Manos del Uruguay
www.fairmountfibers.com

Peace Fleece
www.peacefleece.com

Rowan
www.knitrowan.com

SecureLine
www.lehighgroup.com

Spud & Chloë
www.spudandchloe.com

Needle Felting Supplies
Peace Fleece
www.peacefleece.com

Suede and Leather
Tandy Leather Company
www.tandyleatherfactory.com

Paint-On Soling
Plasti Dip
www.plastidip.com

Castin' Craft Mold Builder
www.eti-usa.com

Beads and Sequins
Michaels
www.michaels.com

JoAnn Fabric and Craft Stores
www.joann.com

A. C. Moore
www.acmoore.com

Hobby Lobby
www.hobbylobby.com

SLIPPERS BY TYPE

Note: All of the slippers in the "Children's" column are sized for children only. Slippers marked with an * in other columns are sized for children and adults.

ACKNOWLEDGMENTS

When I began to work on the proposal for this book, I looked to my shelf of most-favored knitting books for inspiration. The beautiful ones that I returned to again and again, the ones rich with patterns I'd knitted, all shared an editor. I blithely figured I'd submit my proposal to her first and work my way "down" the list of other possible publishers. Imagine my shock and delight when Melanie Falick told me she was interested in this project for STC Craft. It's been a privilege to work with so many talented people throughout this process, and the book you are holding in your hands is the manifestation of the input of those keen eyes and clever minds, but mostly of Melanie's trust in my curiosity. I've learned so much by working with her on this project and am so grateful for the opportunity.

Sue McCain is a gifted technical editor who is also fun to work with. The patterns shine because of her influence and skill. I'm grateful to photographer Mika Nakanishi for creating such a beautiful world for my slippers to live in. It was so exciting to pack up all the slippers and send them to her in Japan so she could shoot them there. It made me happy to hear how the slippers delighted those in her community of friends. Designer Miao Wang gave this book a wonderful spirit and presence, and I'm glad she was able to accompany the slippers on their journey to Japan and take part in the photo shoot.

Thank you to all of the Duo Fiberworks readers and friends; your interest and support delights me every day. Also thank to those who have purchased my knitting patterns over the years. It's a privilege to be a tiny part of your families' lives. Ravelry is my community, storefront, knitting research portal, and source of inspiration. I can't imagine doing this work without it. Diane Gillehand of CraftyPod hooked me up with Kate McKean, my stellar agent, and I'm grateful to both of them.

Many thanks to the yarn companies that graciously provided yarn for this project: Blue Sky Alpacas, Brooklyn Tweed, Brown Sheep Company, Cascade Yarns, Knitting Fever, Malabrigo, Manos del Uruguay, Peace Fleece, Rowan, and Spud & Chloë. I feel fortunate to be surrounded by the talented, thoughtful, and fun women in both my knitting circle and "ladies' meeting": Anne, Meghan, Laura P. , Michelle, Laura W., Andrea, Naomi, Teresa, Heather, Jodie, Michelle, Lisa, Jeneene, and Katlyn. I am truly rich to have friends like you. Hooray for my Tuesday lunch companions: Mary, Nancy, and Carol Ann. The excellent teachers and staff at Berea Community Elementary School teach and care for my previously homeschooled children so I can write and knit; thank you. Laura Wick is my only local knitwear-designer friend and I am grateful for her enthusiasm and encouragement, as well as her helpful suggestions and test-knitting. Johanna Juzwik's insight has been helpful to me through the life of this project.

My extended family has been excited about this project since its inception and supported me in myriad ways: Josh, Megan, Gene, Mary, Josh, Strider, Eli, and Isaac. Judy and John, my mom and dad, made my childhood so rich and continue to delight in all of their children. I'm proud of them and our family. My sister Abby logged hours of phone time with me supporting this project, and I'm grateful for her generous spirit. My twin sister, Laura, contributed uncountable ideas and suggestions over the course of this project. Her eye is as unfailing as her technical skill, and this book is much stronger because of her influence. I'm grateful every day to be her friend and twin. My husband, Michael, is my technology guru, in-house illustrator, and one-man pep squad. Thank you for taking over so many additional responsibilities with grace and love. Thank you to my boys, Julian and Avery: Your cold toes were the reason I began knitting slippers.